Southern

VEGAN

Delicious Down-Home Recipes
for Your Plant-Based Diet

Lauren Hartmann
creator of Rabbit and Wolves

PAGE STREET
PUBLISHING CO.

PAGE STREET
PUBLISHING CO.

First published in 2020 by
Page Street Publishing Co.
27 Congress Street, Suite 105
Salem, MA 01970
www.pagestreetpublishing.com

Distributed by Macmillan, sales in Canada by The Canadian Manda Group.

24 23 22 21   5

ISBN-13: 978-1-62414-982-5
ISBN-10: 1-62414-982-0

Library of Congress Control Number: 2019943012

Cover and book design by Rosie Stewart for Page Street Publishing Co.
Photography by Lauren Hartmann and Julie Grace
Text sub-edited and photography edited by Julie Grace

Printed and bound in China

Page Street Publishing protects our planet by donating to nonprofits like The Trustees, which focuses on local land conservation.

Dedication

For my husband, Chris, who has never and will never
let me fall without being there to catch me.

For my daughter, Lenore, who is the reason I get out of
bed in the morning.

For my dad, Ken, who has always made sure I knew I
could do anything.

For my brother Ethan, who is probably the main reason
I'm doing pretty okay.

Table of Contents

INTRODUCTION

◆

Southern flavors ignite something in us. Certain foods and aromas hold sweet nostalgia and bring delightful memories rushing back, and the colorful stories of our roots are sometimes wrapped up in collard greens and drenched in sweet tea. Whether you've chosen to live the vegan life or you're just looking to incorporate more plant-based recipes into your weekly menu, with this book, you don't have to lose any of those beloved flavors and dishes.

I grew up in a meat-eating household. My parents made food and I ate it without question—until I was about twelve years old. Consuming meat became an issue for me after researching the meat industry for a sixth-grade school assignment. It was the '90s and I had no concept of how to live life without eating meat. I didn't know a single person who was vegetarian, let alone vegan, and I was initially concerned that I'd be missing out on enjoying all the food my family and friends made. My family's roots are southern, and I sure did enjoy eating fried chicken, meatloaf and mashed potatoes. The only vegetables I liked were broccoli and carrots!

While it took me a few more years to really dive into plant-based eating, I stuck with it and now it's just a part of who I am. I don't eat animal products because I love animals and I care a great deal about the planet, but mostly, I just really don't want to confine myself to the standard American diet. And instead of telling others what they shouldn't eat, I prefer to show them the variety of things they can eat on a plant-based diet.

While in culinary school, I was told that I would never get anywhere in my field if I didn't eat meat. However, I stuck to my plant-based values and graduated with a culinary arts degree and a degree in baking and pastry. I eventually began working at a coffee shop where I was put in charge of developing a menu of fresh vegan baked goods. I spent days writing and testing recipes and I realized, damn, I'm good at this. From there, I created The Raven Bakery, my very own vegan baked goods business. But I wanted more. I had so many recipe ideas—not just for sweet treats but savory dishes as well. And so Rabbit and Wolves, my blog baby, was born. It began as a conversation between my husband,

Chris, and I. He's a meat-lover's-pizza kind of guy, so if I could create vegan recipes that made his eyes roll back in his head upon first bite, then I must be onto something worth sharing with the world! We chose the name Rabbit and Wolves to describe me, a rabbit (plant eater), and everyone else in my family, wolves (meat eaters). Dedication to originality is the reason for my blog's success; so much time and energy have gone into creating unique content. All the hard work paid off and now Rabbit and Wolves is my full-time gig, and I couldn't be more satisfied. And it's only getting better!

As a child, my absolute favorite foods were the southern staples I (and many of you) grew up eating. Luckily for all of us, veganism is the future. Many brands now carry vegan butter, and there are more nondairy milks than I can keep track of. Vegan cream cheese and yogurt are abundant. Vegan mayonnaise? No problem! It has never been easier to find all kinds of vegan products, so no matter what food you want to veganize, you can make it happen. Many of those nostalgic recipes from my childhood have been veganized using those ingredients and added to this book just for you. No matter your diet, you will find in these pages the southern-inspired food you've been craving. These recipes not only provide comfort for the soul, they're also a joy to make and to eat. And they're anything but boring. Enjoy!

A Proper
Southern BRUNCH

As a girl who was born and raised in the South and also spent some time living in New York City, brunch might be my favorite thing ever. However, I'm currently distressed by the severe lack of vegan brunch options in my town. Don't get me wrong—I love a bowl of fruit as much as the next gal, but I need something a little more scintillating.

My friends, in this chapter you'll find inspiring brunch options. Recipes that will make you excited to jump out of bed in the morning and declare to the world that you are here, you are important and you deserve a better brunch. You'll find that these southern comfort–inspired brunch recipes are more fun than your typical late-morning meal options. You'll want to devour the Sweet and Spicy Chick'n Biscuits (page 13) immediately. The Giant Gooey Toffee Cinnamon Roll (page 16) is magical and will have all of your friends thinking you are a wizard. No longer will your Sundays be filled with sad bowls of fruit but with genuine brunch magic.

Black Pepper–Chive *Biscuits* and "Sausage" Gravy

The plant-based version of a traditional southern favorite, these mile-high, buttery biscuits are pure magic all on their own. They're also the best biscuits I've ever had, vegan or not. Cover them in tempeh sausage gravy and they become otherworldly. The tempeh sausage is hearty, meaty and smoky, which makes it an excellent substitute for pork.

Serves: 4

Black Pepper–Chive Biscuits

4 cups (480 g) all-purpose flour

4 tsp (16 g) baking powder

1 tsp baking soda

2 tsp (10 g) salt

2 tsp (4 g) black pepper

1½ cups (360 ml) nondairy milk

1 tsp apple cider vinegar

½ cup (120 g) cold vegan butter

½ cup (120 g) solid coconut oil

¼ cup (25 g) finely chopped fresh chives

Olive oil, as needed

Preheat the oven to 450°F (232°C). Spray a medium baking sheet with nonstick spray.

To make the black pepper–chive biscuits, sift together the flour, baking powder and baking soda in a large bowl. Stir in the salt and black pepper.

In a small bowl, whisk together the milk and vinegar. Set the mixture aside for 1 minute to thicken.

Meanwhile, break the butter and coconut oil into small pieces with your hands and drop the pieces into the flour mixture.

Using a fork or your fingers, press and pinch the butter and coconut oil into the flour until the flour resembles sand. Add the chives.

Pour the milk and vinegar mixture into the flour mixture, stirring to combine. When the mixture gets too hard to stir, knead it with your hands for about 1 minute until a smooth ball of dough forms.

Transfer the dough to a floured surface and pat it out flat. Fold the dough over, then pat it out, then fold it over again. Pat it out, then roll the dough out until it is ½ to 1 inch (13 mm to 2.5 cm) thick.

Cut the dough into circles with a cookie cutter or cup. You should get about 8 large biscuits.

Place the biscuits on the prepared baking sheet up against each other. (If they are all touching, they will rise more.)

Brush the tops of the biscuits with the olive oil and bake for 15 to 18 minutes, or until they are golden brown and baked through.

(Continued)

"SAUSAGE" GRAVY

1 tbsp (15 ml) olive oil

8 oz (240 g) tempeh

Salt, to taste

Black pepper, to taste

2 tsp (10 ml) soy sauce or coconut aminos

1 tsp liquid smoke

¼ cup (60 g) vegan butter

¼ cup (30 g) all-purpose flour

2 cups (480 ml) almond milk or other nondairy milk

While the biscuits bake, make the "sausage" gravy. Heat the olive oil in a large nonstick skillet over medium-high heat.

Crumble the tempeh into small sausage-like pieces, then add them to the skillet. Season the tempeh with salt and black pepper. Sauté until the tempeh crumbles are brown, 5 to 7 minutes.

Add the soy sauce and liquid smoke. Toss to combine and sauté for 1 to 2 minutes. Transfer the tempeh crumbles to a medium bowl and set it aside.

Add the butter to the skillet and melt it over medium-low heat. Once the butter has melted, add the flour and whisk to combine and make a roux. Simmer the roux for 1 to 2 minutes to thicken and brown a bit.

Add the milk and whisk to combine with the roux, making sure there are no lumps. Season with a few pinches of salt and black pepper. Simmer the gravy, whisking frequently for 2 to 3 minutes, or until the gravy is thick.

Add the tempeh crumbles to the gravy. Stir to combine. Taste and adjust the seasonings, as needed.

When the biscuits are done, cut a biscuit open on a plate and cover it with about ¼ cup (60 g) of gravy.

Sweet and Spicy Chick'n *Biscuits*

What's the most beautiful sight you will ever see? A southern staple, deliciously veganized! This recipe uses chick'n, which is pretty close to the real thing—but cruelty-free. These baked patties are crispy, with a delightful texture to satisfy your traditional southern food cravings, and they are served in fluffy "buttermilk" biscuits and drizzled with a spicy maple syrup. So rise and shine, because life is grand!

Serves: 8

Chick'n Patties

1 (15-oz [450-g]) can white beans, drained and rinsed

1 tbsp (15 ml) olive oil

⅓ cup (80 ml) vegetable broth

2 tbsp (30 ml) soy sauce

1 cup (144 g) vital wheat gluten

⅓ cup (18 g) plus ½ cup (28 g) panko breadcrumbs, divided

1 tsp salt

Pinch of cayenne pepper

½ cup (45 g) plain vegan breadcrumbs

Preheat the oven to 400°F (204°C). Spray a medium baking sheet with nonstick spray and set it aside.

To make the chick'n patties, place the white beans in a large bowl and smash the beans completely with a fork or potato masher.

Add the oil, broth and soy sauce to the beans. Whisk to combine.

Add the vital wheat gluten, ⅓ cup (18 g) of the panko breadcrumbs, salt and cayenne pepper to the beans. Stir to combine, and when the mixture gets too hard to stir, knead it with your hands. Knead for 1 minute, just to bring everything together, and form a ball of dough.

Break the dough into 8 pieces.

In a small bowl, stir together the remaining ½ cup (28 g) of the panko breadcrumbs and the plain breadcrumbs.

Roll each piece of chick'n into a ball, then flatten it slightly into a patty. Press the patty into the bowl with the breadcrumbs, coating each side.

Put the patties on the prepared baking sheet. Spray the tops of the patties with more nonstick spray.

(Continued)

Sweet and Spicy Chick'n Biscuits (Continued)

"BUTTERMILK" BISCUITS

4 cups (480 g) all-purpose flour

4 tsp (16 g) baking powder

1 tsp baking soda

2 tsp (10 g) salt

1½ cups (360 ml) soy milk

1 tsp fresh lemon juice

¾ cup (180 g) cold vegetable shortening

Olive oil, as needed

SPICY MAPLE SYRUP

½ cup (120 ml) pure maple syrup

1–2 tsp (5–10 ml) hot sauce

Bake the patties for 15 minutes, flip them and bake for 15 minutes more.

While the chick'n patties bake, make the biscuits. Spray another medium baking sheet with nonstick spray and set it aside.

In a large bowl, sift together the flour, baking powder and baking soda. Stir in the salt.

In a small bowl, whisk together the milk and lemon juice. Let this mixture sit for 3 to 5 minutes to thicken.

Break the shortening up into small pieces with your fingers and drop the shortening into the flour mixture. Using a fork or your fingers, press and pinch the shortening into the flour, making sure it is evenly distributed and the flour resembles sand.

Pour the milk mixture into the flour mixture and stir. Knead for 1 minute with your hands, until the dough is smooth and no longer sticky.

Transfer the dough to a floured surface, then press the dough out and fold it over. Press it out again and roll it out until it is about ½ inch (13 mm) thick. Cut 8 circles out of the dough with a cookie cutter or cup. Put the biscuits up against one another on the prepared baking sheet so their sides are touching.

Brush the tops of the biscuits with the oil and put the baking sheet in the fridge until the chick'n patties are done.

When the chick'n patties are done, remove them from the oven and increase the oven temperature to 450°F (232°C). (To keep the chick'n warm, keep it on top of the oven.)

Bake the biscuits for 12 to 15 minutes, or until they are golden brown.

To make the spicy maple syrup, whisk together the maple syrup and hot sauce in a small bowl.

Cut open a biscuit, then drizzle it with about ½ tablespoon (8 ml) of the spicy maple syrup. Top the biscuit with a chick'n patty, drizzle it with another ½ tablespoon (8 ml) of spicy maple syrup, then top the patty with the other half of the biscuit.

GIANT GOOEY TOFFEE *Cinnamon Roll*

Welcome. You are about to meet the most glorious brunch item the world has ever seen: a gigantic cinnamon roll you can cut like a cake. The moist yet fluffy roll is baked on top of gooey toffee, drizzled with icing and ready to make you happy to be alive.

Serves: 6

DOUGH

½ cup (120 ml) water

1¾ cups (420 ml) soy milk or other nondairy milk

¼ cup (60 g) vegan butter

2¼ tsp (7 g) active dry yeast

⅓ cup (64 g) vegan granulated sugar

4½ cups (540 g) all-purpose flour, plus more as needed

1 tsp baking powder

1½ tsp (8 g) salt

TOFFEE

½ cup (120 g) vegan butter

¼ cup (48 g) vegan granulated sugar

¼ cup (36 g) vegan brown sugar

2 tbsp (30 ml) water

To make the dough, combine the water, milk and butter in a small saucepan over medium-low heat. Heat just until the butter has melted and the water and milk are warm, about 110°F (43°C), about 2 to 3 minutes. (The liquid should feel warm to the touch, but it should not burn you.)

Add the liquid to a large bowl or the bowl of a stand mixer fitted with a dough hook attachment.

Sprinkle the yeast into the liquid, then sprinkle the sugar on top of the yeast. Let the yeast bloom for 5 minutes. The yeast will make large bubbles on top of the liquid.

Sift together the flour, baking powder and salt in a large bowl.

Add the flour mixture to the milk mixture, 1 cup (120 g) at a time, stirring or using a dough hook to combine. Once all the flour mixture has been added, knead the dough with your hands—or using the dough hook, knead for 1 minute in the stand mixer—until the dough forms a smooth ball, adding a few pinches of flour at a time until the dough is no longer sticky.

Cover the dough with a kitchen towel and let it rise in a warm place for 1 hour.

Right before the dough is ready, make the toffee. In a small saucepan over medium heat, combine the butter, granulated sugar, brown sugar and water. Whisk to combine once the butter has melted. Reduce the heat to low and simmer the mixture for 2 to 3 minutes to thicken it slightly.

Pour the toffee into the bottom of an 8-inch (20-cm) springform pan. Swirl the pan around to spread out the toffee evenly. Set the toffee aside to cool.

Preheat the oven to 325°F (163°C).

FILLING

¾ cup (180 g) room-temperature vegan butter

¾ cup (108 g) vegan brown sugar

1½ tbsp (14 g) ground cinnamon

ICING

2 tbsp (30 g) vegan butter

2 tbsp (30 g) vegetable shortening

2 tbsp (30 ml) nondairy milk

1 cup (130 g) vegan powdered sugar

1 tsp pure vanilla extract

Pinch of salt

Once the dough has doubled in size, transfer it to a floured surface. Roll the dough out to a ¼-inch (6-mm)-thick rectangle.

To make the filling, spread the entire surface of the dough with the room-temperature butter, then sprinkle the brown sugar and cinnamon evenly on top of the dough.

Cut the dough into long 2-inch (5-cm)-wide strips. Stack the strips on top of one another, and then roll them into the shape of one giant cinnamon roll.

Put the cinnamon roll into the springform pan, on top of the toffee. Let the cinnamon roll sit for about 5 minutes to rise again in the pan.

Bake the cinnamon roll for 30 minutes. Cover the top of the roll with foil, then bake for 15 minutes more, or until the cinnamon roll is golden brown and cooked through.

Let the cinnamon roll cool while you make the icing. In a small bowl, whisk together the butter, shortening, milk, powdered sugar, vanilla and salt until smooth.

Drizzle the icing over the cinnamon roll. To serve, you can flip the cinnamon roll over and serve it toffee side up or cut it and serve it with the toffee on the bottom.

*See photo on page 8.

DINER-STYLE *Home Fries*

Once upon a time, I was a child. A child who begged my dad to make his special home fries every weekend. They took time and love. He slow-cooked the onions and potatoes into sweet and salty, caramelized magic. Those home fries were my favorite thing in the world, and these little potatoes are an ode to his labor of love. This recipe tastes just as good, but takes half the time by par-boiling the potatoes. However, all the love is still there!

Serves: 2 to 3

1 lb (450 g) russet potatoes, cut into ½-inch (13-mm) cubes

2 tbsp (30 ml) olive oil

1 medium Vidalia onion, diced

2 tbsp (30 g) vegan butter

1 tsp garlic powder

½ tsp seasoned salt

Salt, to taste

Black pepper, to taste

Scallions, for topping

Add the potatoes to a large pot of cold water. Bring the potatoes to a boil over high heat and boil for 5 minutes, reducing the heat as needed. The potatoes should be a little tender but not cooked all the way. Drain the potatoes.

While the potatoes are boiling, heat the oil in a large cast-iron or nonstick skillet over medium-high heat.

Add the onion to the skillet and reduce the heat to medium-low. Sauté for about 15 minutes, or until the onion is light brown.

Add the potatoes to the skillet. Add the butter, garlic powder, seasoned salt, salt and black pepper on top of the potatoes. Toss to coat the potatoes in the seasonings.

Using a spatula, press the potatoes into the bottom of the skillet in a single layer. Cook the potatoes, undisturbed, for 5 minutes. Toss the potatoes, press them back into the skillet in a single layer and cook, undisturbed, for another 5 minutes. Repeat this process until the potatoes are all brown and cooked through, 15 to 20 minutes. Taste and adjust the seasonings. Top with scallions.

Serve the home fries as a side with Sweet and Spicy Chick'n Biscuits (page 13) or Pecan Pie French Toast (page 23).

CRAZY-FLUFFY BUTTERMILK SHEET PAN *Pancakes*

Have you ever woken up on a Sunday, sat up and rubbed your eyes, wishing for pillowy pancakes, smothered in maple syrup, to magically appear? Enter these sheet pan pancakes. It takes five minutes to whip up this plant-based, refined sugar–free "buttermilk" pancake batter and fifteen minutes to bake the pancakes in the oven. Boom! Your wish is my command.

Serves: 6 to 8

3 cups (720 ml) soy milk or other nondairy milk

1 tbsp (15 ml) apple cider vinegar

3 cups (360 g) all-purpose flour

3 tbsp (36 g) baking powder

1 tsp salt

1 tbsp (15 ml) pure vanilla extract

½ cup (120 ml) pure maple syrup, plus more as needed

⅓ cup (80 ml) vegetable oil

Sliced fresh strawberries (optional), for serving

Grated vegan chocolate (optional), for serving

Coconut Whipped Cream (page 151) or store-bought vegan whipped cream (optional), for serving

Preheat the oven to 400°F (204°C). Spray an 11 x 7–inch (28 x 18–cm) rimmed baking sheet with nonstick spray.

To make the pancakes, whisk together the milk and vinegar in a medium bowl. Set the bowl aside to let the mixture thicken and curdle slightly to create vegan buttermilk.

In a large bowl, sift the flour and baking powder together. Stir in the salt. Set the bowl aside.

Whisk the vanilla, maple syrup and oil into the buttermilk.

Pour the buttermilk mixture into the flour mixture a little at a time, whisking constantly, until all of the buttermilk mixture is incorporated.

Then, pour the batter into the prepared rimmed baking sheet. Smooth the batter out evenly.

Bake the pancake for 15 to 20 minutes, or until golden brown and a toothpick inserted into the center comes out clean.

Let the pancake cool for 1 minute, then cut it into squares and serve it with the strawberries, chocolate and Coconut Whipped Cream (if using).

PECAN PIE *French Toast*

Pecan pie screams, "Look at me, y'all, I'm southern!" So I can't think of any better way to make the ultimate southern brunch complete. This is a baked French toast, which is the best kind in my opinion. It is baked on top of brown sugar, vegan butter and pecans, creating a caramel and pecan crust that is beyond amazing.

Serves: 6 to 8

2 cups (480 ml) nondairy milk

2 tbsp (14 g) flax meal

2 tbsp (16 g) all-purpose flour

1 tbsp (15 ml) pure vanilla extract

4 tbsp (60 ml) pure maple syrup, divided, plus more for serving (optional)

Pinch of salt

¼ cup (60 g) vegan butter, melted

½ cup (72 g) vegan brown sugar

1 cup (120 g) finely chopped roasted and salted pecans

6–8 (½-inch [13-mm]-thick) slices crusty bread (such as sourdough)

Coconut Whipped Cream (page 151) or store-bought vegan whipped cream (optional), for serving

Preheat the oven to 350°F (177°C).

In a large bowl, whisk together the milk, flax meal, flour, vanilla, 2 tablespoons (30 ml) of the maple syrup and salt. Set the mixture aside.

Pour the butter into the bottom of a 13 x 9–inch (33 x 23–cm) baking dish, spreading the butter around so that it evenly coats the bottom of the baking dish.

Sprinkle the brown sugar over the butter. Make sure the brown sugar covers the entire bottom of the baking dish.

Sprinkle the pecans over the brown sugar. Drizzle the remaining 2 tablespoons (30 ml) of maple syrup over the pecans.

Figure out how many slices of bread will fit in a single layer in the baking dish. (Generally, 6 to 8 slices will fit nicely.)

Put the slices of bread into the milk mixture. Let them soak for 2 to 3 minutes so they can absorb the liquid.

Place the bread in a single layer on top of the pecans in the baking dish.

Bake for 35 to 45 minutes, or until the bread is baked through and the pecan topping is brown and bubbly.

Let the French toast cool for 5 to 7 minutes so the pecan topping can harden.

To serve, use a spatula to scoop a slice of toast out of the baking dish and flip it over so the pecans face upward. Top the French toast with additional maple syrup (if using) and Coconut Whipped Cream (if using).

BLACKBERRY COBBLER *Yogurt*

I've searched far and wide for vegan yogurt that I actually love. In pursuit of excellence, this brilliant blackberry cobbler yogurt was born! My homemade, sugar-free version has it all. It's thick and creamy, lightly sweet and crunchy. This healthy breakfast really hits the spot with its blackberry compote and cobbler crumble.

Serves: 4

VANILLA YOGURT

1 (15-oz [450-g]) block firm tofu

1 (14-oz [420-ml]) can full-fat coconut milk or coconut cream

¼ cup (60 ml) pure maple syrup, plus more for serving (optional)

1 tsp pure vanilla extract

4 vegan probiotic capsules

COBBLER CRUMBLES

1 cup (120 g) all-purpose flour

½ cup (40 g) rolled oats

1 tsp ground cinnamon

Pinch of salt

⅓ cup (80 ml) pure maple syrup

3 tbsp (45 g) solid coconut oil

BLACKBERRY COMPOTE

2 cups (288 g) fresh blackberries

3 tbsp (45 ml) pure maple syrup

1 tsp fresh lemon juice

To make the vanilla yogurt, drain the tofu and squeeze out as much of its liquid as you can with your hands.

In a blender, combine the tofu, coconut milk, maple syrup and vanilla. Open up the probiotic capsules and pour the powder into the blender. Blend on high, scraping down the sides as needed, until the yogurt is silky smooth. (It will be thin, but it will thicken as it chills.)

Transfer the yogurt to a medium bowl then put the yogurt in the fridge to chill for at least 3 hours or overnight. The longer the yogurt chills, the thicker it will get.

To make the cobbler crumbles, preheat the oven to 400°F (204°C). Spray a medium baking sheet with nonstick spray.

In a medium bowl, stir together the flour, oats, cinnamon and salt. Pour in the maple syrup, stirring to combine.

Break the coconut oil up into pieces with your fingers and drop them into the bowl. Using your fingers, press and pinch the coconut oil into the flour mixture to form crumbles. Spread the crumbles out on the prepared baking sheet.

Bake the crumbles for 5 minutes. Toss them and bake for another 3 to 5 minutes, or until they are golden brown.

While the crumbles are baking, make the blackberry compote.

Combine the blackberries, maple syrup and lemon juice in a small saucepan over medium-low heat. Simmer for 5 to 10 minutes, or until the blackberries are soft and you can smash them. Set the compote aside to cool.

When the crumbles are done, let them cool for about 5 minutes. In a small bowl, layer the yogurt with the crumbles and drizzle the top with the blackberry compote. Serve the yogurt with additional maple syrup drizzled on top for a sweeter dish, if desired.

CINNAMON STREUSEL PEACH *Bread*

Once in a lifetime, a breakfast bread comes around that is so delicious, so moist, so flavorful that no other breakfast baked good will ever do again. This summertime treat is simple and so, so yummy! Cinnamon and peaches are a match made in food heaven, and this bread proves it.

Serves: 6 to 8

PEACH BREAD

½ cup (120 g) room-temperature vegan butter

½ cup (120 ml) pure maple syrup

½ cup (123 g) unsweetened applesauce

1 tsp pure vanilla extract

2 cups (240 g) all-purpose flour

2 tsp (8 g) baking powder

1 tsp baking soda

1 tsp ground cinnamon

1 tsp salt

¼ cup (60 ml) nondairy milk

2 cups (450 g) diced firm peaches

STREUSEL TOPPING

¼ cup (30 g) all-purpose flour

¼ cup (36 g) vegan brown sugar

¼ cup (48 g) vegan granulated sugar

1 tsp ground cinnamon

½ tsp salt

2 tbsp (30 g) room-temperature vegan butter

To make the bread, preheat the oven to 350°F (177°C). Spray an 8 x 4–inch (20 x 10–cm) loaf pan with nonstick spray.

In a large bowl, mix together the butter, maple syrup, applesauce and vanilla using an electric hand mixer or whisk. Set the bowl aside.

In another medium bowl, sift together the flour, baking powder, baking soda and cinnamon. Add the salt and stir to combine.

Add the flour mixture to the butter mixture a little at a time, stirring to combine.

Add the milk, stirring to combine. Fold the peaches into the batter.

Pour the batter into the prepared loaf pan. Smooth it out evenly. Set the pan aside.

To make the streusel topping, whisk together the flour, brown sugar, granulated sugar, cinnamon and salt. Add the butter, breaking it apart and mixing it into the flour mixture with your hands. Press the butter into the flour mixture until it is evenly distributed and the mixture is crumbly.

Sprinkle the streusel topping on top of the peach batter.

Bake for 35 to 45 minutes, or until a toothpick inserted into the center comes out clean.

Let the bread cool completely before slicing.

Hot Tip: This bread is delicious the next day toasted and slathered with vegan butter and drizzled with maple syrup.

Hummingbird Breakfast *Cake*

Cake for breakfast is no longer just a sweet dream—you can still be a responsible adult and enjoy this take on a southern classic dessert for breakfast! It is totally refined sugar–free, and it's filled with bananas, pineapple and pecans. It is true perfection, and it may even make you excited to get up in the morning. Living in the South, I have had a lot of hummingbird cake in my life, and I have to say this one might be my favorite. Yes, it is healthier and incredible.

Serves: 6

1½ cups (180 g) all-purpose flour

1 tsp baking powder

½ tsp baking soda

1 tsp ground cinnamon

1 tsp salt

½ cup (80 g) rolled oats

1 large ripe banana

½ cup (120 ml) pure maple syrup, plus more for serving

½ cup (120 ml) vegetable oil

1 tsp pure vanilla extract

½ cup (120 ml) nondairy milk

1 cup (165 g) coarsely chopped fresh pineapple

1 cup (120 g) finely chopped roasted pecans

Vegan butter, for serving

Preheat the oven to 350°F (177°C). Spray an 8-inch (20-cm) round cake pan with nonstick spray.

In a large bowl, sift together the flour, baking powder, baking soda and cinnamon. Add the salt and oats and stir to combine. Set the mixture aside.

Mash the banana completely in a medium bowl. Add the maple syrup, oil, vanilla and milk and whisk to combine.

Pour the banana mixture into the flour mixture. Whisk to fully combine.

Fold the pineapple and pecans into the batter.

Pour the batter into the prepared cake pan. Spread the batter out evenly.

Bake the cake for 20 to 30 minutes, or until a toothpick inserted into the center comes out clean.

Let the cake cool completely then serve with a drizzle of maple syrup, or toast slices of the cake the next day and slather them with butter.

SPICED APPLE PIE OVERNIGHT *Oats*

I don't know about you, but I forget to eat breakfast all the time. Solution? Something that is ready to eat right when I get up. Most overnight oats I have had are incredibly boring, but not these. These oats are easy, healthy and a great on-the-go breakfast or brunch. I like to put my oats in little jars and grab one as I'm running out the door. I may forget to brush my hair, and I may put my shirt on backwards, but dang it, I have breakfast!

Serves: 2

½ cup (40 g) rolled oats

1 tsp chia seeds

1 tsp apple pie spice

⅓ cup (82 g) unsweetened applesauce

1 cup (240 ml) almond milk or other nondairy milk

1 cup (120 g) diced Fuji or Gala apples

2 tbsp (30 ml) pure maple syrup

¼ tsp ground ginger

½ tsp ground cinnamon

½ tsp pure vanilla extract

The night before you want to serve the overnight oats, stir together the oats, chia seeds and apple pie spice in a medium bowl.

Add the applesauce and milk. Stir to combine.

Cover the bowl and refrigerate it overnight (or for at least 8 hours). The oats will get thicker the longer they sit.

In a small saucepan over medium-high heat, combine the apples, maple syrup, ginger, cinnamon and vanilla, tossing to coat all the apples. Cook the apples for 5 to 10 minutes, until they are soft and the sauce has thickened slightly. Remove the saucepan from the heat.

Let the apples cool completely, transfer them to a lidded container and put them in the fridge as well.

In the morning, put the oats in a jar or bowl and top them with the apple topping.

Hot Tip: If I have time in the morning, I like to make the apple topping right before I am ready to eat. Then I serve the cold oats with the hot apples. It's a delicious combo!

Easy as ALL *Get-Out*

Sometimes I just want to cook all day, making a million different components for one meal and zoning out while I chop vegetables. The recipes in this chapter are for the other 364 days a year when I just want to eat something delicious that also happens to be quick and easy. Simplified vegan versions of your favorite southern comfort foods can be found here: gumbo, cheesy grits, pot roast and more! These crazy-easy meals are perfect for all our busy days. You know, the "I gotta get something awesome on the table right *now*" kinda days.

If you need a dump-everything-in-one-pot meal, check out the rich and unique flavor of the Cowboy Chili (page 57). Looking for a throw-this-and-that-in-the-oven sorta thing? I've got you covered with the Blackened Tofu and Coleslaw Sandwiches (page 50). So get acquainted with your new go-to weeknight meals—they're proof that easy and delicious can go hand in hand.

My Very Favorite *Gumbo*

Of course my very favorite gumbo features Cajun-spiced, crispy roasted potatoes. Because . . . why the heck not? Pour a few giant spoonfuls of this perfect gumbo over some potatoes and rice if you are a double-carb person like me. Top it with vegan sausages if you want, and prepare to call this your very favorite gumbo.

Serves: 6

Gumbo

2 tbsp (30 ml) olive oil

6 cloves garlic, finely chopped

1 large jalapeño, diced

2 large carrots, diced

½ medium white onion, diced

1 large rib celery, diced

1 medium red or green bell pepper, diced

Salt, as needed

1 (14-oz [420-g]) can roasted tomatoes, undrained

5 cups (1.2 L) vegetable broth, divided

2 tbsp (18 g) Cajun seasoning

¼ cup (60 g) vegan butter

¼ cup (30 g) all-purpose flour

Black pepper, to taste

Cooked rice (optional)

Sliced and pan-fried vegan sausages (optional)

Cajun-Spiced Potatoes

1 lb (450 g) russet potatoes, diced

1 tbsp (15 ml) olive oil

1 tbsp (9 g) Cajun seasoning

Preheat the oven to 400°F (204°C).

To make the gumbo, heat the oil in a large pot over medium-high heat. Add the garlic, jalapeño, carrots, onion, celery and bell pepper. Season the vegetables with a pinch of salt and sauté for about 10 minutes, until the onion and celery are translucent and the carrots are soft.

Once the onion is translucent and the other vegetables are starting to brown, add the tomatoes, 4 cups (960 ml) of the broth and Cajun seasoning.

Bring the mixture to a simmer, reduce the heat to low and simmer for 15 to 20 minutes to develop the flavors and finish cooking the vegetables.

While the gumbo is simmering, make the Cajun-spiced potatoes. Put the potatoes on a medium-sized baking sheet, drizzle them with the oil and sprinkle them with the Cajun seasoning. Toss to coat all the potatoes and roast in the oven for 20 to 25 minutes, or until they are brown and crispy.

Once the gumbo has simmered for about 15 minutes, heat the butter in a small saucepan over medium-high heat. Once the butter has melted, add the flour. Whisk to combine and form a roux. Simmer the roux for 1 to 2 minutes.

Whisk in the remaining 1 cup (240 ml) of broth with the roux, making sure there are no lumps. Reduce the heat to low and simmer for 2 to 3 minutes, or until the mixture is thick.

Add the roux to the gumbo and whisk to combine. Simmer the gumbo for about 5 minutes to thicken. Taste and adjust the seasonings with additional salt and the black pepper.

Serve the gumbo with the potatoes over the rice (if using) and topped with the sausages (if using).

SPICY OVEN-FRIED *Tofu*

How do you get that most perfect tofu you've been longing for—tender and flavorful on the inside, extremely crispy and crunchy on the outside—without frying? Well, stick with me, kid! I'm here for you and so is this oven-fried tofu. It's the perfect centerpiece for all your southern feasts. I love to serve this tofu with Creamy Garlic-Truffle Grits (page 102), Chili Smashed Potato Salad (page 106) and Dill Pickle Pasta Salad (page 114). Go ahead, put out a big ol' bucket of this tofu—you'll be the most popular one at the party!

Serves: 4

1 (15-oz [450-g]) block extra-firm tofu, pressed (see sidebar)

2 cups (480 ml) nondairy milk

¼ cup (60 ml) plus 1 tsp hot sauce, divided

2 tsp (10 ml) agave syrup

2 tsp (10 g) salt, divided

1¼ cups (188 g) cornstarch

1 tsp chili powder

3 cups (75 g) cornflakes, crushed, gluten-free if desired (see Hot Tip)

⅓ cup (80 ml) pure maple syrup

Hot Tip: I like to pulse the cornflakes in my food processor to crush them. Or I put them in a large zip-top bag and smash them with a rolling pin until they are finely crushed. The finer the cornflakes, the easier it is to get them to stick to the tofu.

Cut the block of tofu into 6 to 8 large triangles.

In a medium bowl, whisk together the milk, ¼ cup (60 ml) of the hot sauce, the agave syrup and 1 teaspoon of the salt.

Put the tofu triangles into the bowl and let them marinate for at least 1 hour (the longer, the better).

Preheat the oven to 400°F (204°C). Spray a medium baking sheet with nonstick spray.

Line up 2 large bowls next to the bowl containing the tofu, to create a dredging station. To the first bowl, add the cornstarch, the remaining 1 teaspoon of salt and the chili powder. Stir to combine. Place the crushed cornflakes in the second bowl.

Take a piece of tofu out of the marinade, put the tofu into the cornstarch and coat it completely. Dip the tofu back into the marinade, coating it completely. Dredge it again in the cornstarch, coat it again in the marinade, then coat it in the cornflakes. Press the cornflakes onto the tofu to coat it completely. Place the tofu on the prepared baking sheet.

Repeat the preceding steps with all of the tofu pieces. Spray the top of the tofu with nonstick spray.

Bake the tofu for 15 minutes, then flip it and bake for 15 to 20 minutes, or until the tofu is crispy.

While the tofu is baking, whisk together the maple syrup and remaining 1 teaspoon of hot sauce in a small bowl.

When the tofu is done, drizzle the tofu with the spicy maple syrup and serve immediately.

Tips for Pressing Tofu

- Always select extra-firm or super-firm tofu for savory dishes. To prep the tofu, drain the liquid from the package, then place the block of tofu on a plate and sprinkle it with salt. Rub the salt over the entire block. This not only helps season it but also draws out more moisture.

- Line a plate with paper towels or a clean kitchen towel and place the tofu on top. Put more paper towels or another kitchen towel on top of the tofu.

- Put something heavy on top of the tofu. I like to put a small baking sheet on top and then add books or cans to weigh it down.

- Let the tofu sit beneath the heavy objects for at least 30 minutes. Once the tofu has lost most of its moisture and become much firmer, it is ready.

THE BEST DANG *Hot Fries*

If you have never heard of hot fries, welcome! I'm about to make your life significantly better. Traditionally, hot fries are French fries topped with a cheese sauce that is flavored like Nashville hot sauce. Obviously, I had to make my own vegan version, and I mean, come on—these are the greatest cheese fries. Sweet, spicy and creamy, the roux-thickened nondairy cheese sauce in this recipe simulates the real deal perfectly with just some nutritional yeast and mustard.

Serves: 4 to 6

24 oz (720 g) frozen vegan French fries

2 tbsp (30 g) vegan butter

2 tbsp (16 g) all-purpose flour

1½ cups (360 ml) nondairy milk

3 tbsp (12 g) nutritional yeast

2 tbsp (30 ml) hot sauce

2 tbsp (30 ml) agave syrup or pure maple syrup

1 tsp Dijon mustard

1 tsp garlic powder

1 tsp paprika

Salt, to taste

Finely chopped fresh chives, as needed

Bake the French fries according to the package's directions.

While the fries are baking, make the hot cheese sauce. Heat the butter in a large skillet over medium heat. Once the butter has melted, whisk the flour into the butter to make a roux. Cook for 1 minute to thicken the roux.

Add the milk and whisk vigorously to combine it with the roux. Make sure there are no lumps.

Add the nutritional yeast, hot sauce, agave syrup, mustard, garlic powder, paprika and salt. Whisk to combine and bring the cheese sauce to a simmer. Reduce the heat to low and simmer, whisking frequently, until the sauce has thickened, about 5 minutes. Taste and adjust the seasonings. Keep the sauce warm over low heat until the fries are done.

When the fries are done, pour the cheese sauce over the fries and sprinkle them with the chives.

Fried Broccoli WITH Creole Rémoulade

Broccoli is probably my favorite vegetable. What makes it even better? Frying it, obviously. This light and crispy breaded broccoli is super easy and served with a tangy, spicy Creole sauce. This recipe is for a whole head of broccoli, and you'll be very happy that you made that much. I love to serve this as an appetizer or a side with some Baked White Mac and Cheese (page 96) or Barbecue Tempeh and Sweet Corn Pudding (page 65).

Serves: 4

CREOLE RÉMOULADE

1 cup (220 g) vegan mayo

1 tbsp (15 ml) hot sauce

2 tbsp (32 g) Dijon mustard

1 tsp fresh lemon juice

2 cloves garlic, finely chopped

1 tsp paprika

1 tsp agave syrup

Pinch of salt

Pinch of cayenne pepper

FRIED BROCCOLI

1 cup (240 ml) almond milk or other nondairy milk

1 tsp apple cider vinegar

¾ cup (90 g) all-purpose flour

½ cup (75 g) cornstarch

1 tsp salt

2 cups (110 g) panko breadcrumbs

1 small head broccoli, cut into 1-inch (2.5-cm) florets

Vegetable oil, as needed

Finely chopped fresh chives, as needed

To make the Creole rémoulade, combine the mayo, hot sauce, mustard, lemon juice, garlic, paprika, agave syrup, salt and cayenne pepper in a small bowl. Whisk to combine and set the bowl aside.

To make the fried broccoli, whisk together the milk and vinegar in a small bowl. Set the bowl aside.

In a large bowl, sift together the flour and cornstarch. Stir in the salt.

Pour the milk mixture into the flour mixture. Whisk until smooth and fully combined. The batter should be thick.

Pour the breadcrumbs into a medium bowl.

Dip a broccoli floret into the batter, coating it completely. Then put the broccoli into the breadcrumbs and coat it completely. Place the coated broccoli on a baking sheet. Repeat this process with the remainder of the broccoli.

In a large skillet over medium-high heat, bring about ½ inch (13 mm) of oil to 350°F (177°C). Small bubbles will form in the oil when it is hot enough.

Add some of the broccoli florets, making sure not to crowd the skillet. Fry the broccoli on each side, reducing the heat as needed, for 2 to 4 minutes per side, or until the broccoli is brown and crispy. Repeat this process with the remainder of the broccoli.

Serve the fried broccoli immediately, drizzled with the Creole rémoulade and topped with the chives. Serve extra rémoulade on the side.

Hot Tip: If you are not a fan of frying veggies, you can bake this broccoli. It will still get nice and crispy. Bake the broccoli at 425°F (218°C) for about 10 minutes. Flip the broccoli and bake for another 5 minutes, or until it is crispy.

CREAMY WHITE BEAN *Chili*

I'll be honest—many times, when I come up with a recipe, I'm all like, "Dang, I'm smart." But I think the decision to make a cream sauce out of white beans is one of my best ideas yet! Inspired by a usually heavy, high-calorie meal, I have turned this ultimate comfort food into something pretty healthy. Normal white chili features heavy cream and cheese. My version has veggie broth and beans, but I promise it will knock your socks off.

Serves: 4

3 (15-oz [450-g]) cans navy, cannellini or great northern beans, drained, divided

1½ cups (360 ml) vegetable broth, divided

1 tbsp (15 ml) olive oil

½ medium yellow onion, diced

4 cloves garlic, finely chopped

Pinch plus 1 tsp salt, divided

Pinch plus ½ tsp black pepper, divided

8 oz (240 g) canned diced green chiles, plus more as needed (optional)

1 tsp ground cumin

Pinch of chili powder

Pinch of cayenne pepper

Finely chopped fresh chives (optional)

Vegan sour cream (optional)

Pickled jalapeños (optional)

Add 1 can of the beans to a blender. Add ½ cup (120 ml) of the broth and blend on high until the beans are completely smooth. Set the white bean cream aside.

Heat the oil in a large pot over medium-high heat. Add the onion and garlic. Sauté for 3 to 5 minutes, or until the onion is translucent, reducing the heat if needed to prevent burning.

Add the remaining 2 cans of beans to the pot. Stir and season the mixture with the pinch of salt and pinch of black pepper.

Add the green chiles to the pot, stirring to combine. Sauté for 1 to 2 minutes.

Add the remaining 1 cup (240 ml) of broth, the white bean cream, the remaining 1 teaspoon of salt, cumin, the remaining ½ teaspoon of black pepper, chili powder and cayenne pepper to the pot. Stir to combine and reduce the heat to low. Simmer, uncovered, for 10 to 15 minutes, or until the chili has thickened slightly.

Taste and adjust the seasonings. Serve the chili with chives (if using), sour cream (if using), pickled jalapeños (if using) or more green chiles (if using).

SOUTHERN FAUX *Fish and Chips*

My family spent many a summer in Kentucky when I was a kid. There, we would attend at least one good fish fry. Hushpuppies and cornmeal-crusted catfish were abundant. Marinate, score with a knife, crust and fry some tofu and you have an amazing representation of what you can experience at a good old-fashioned fish fry.

Serves: 3 to 4

SOUTHERN FAUX FISH

1 (16-oz [480-g]) block extra-firm or super-firm tofu, pressed (see page 37)

1 cup (240 ml) almond milk

2 tsp (10 ml) fresh lemon juice

Pinch of salt, plus more as needed

Pinch of black pepper

Pinch of cayenne pepper

1½ cups (255 g) cornmeal

½ cup (60 g) all-purpose flour

1 tsp Old Bay Seasoning, plus more as needed

2 tsp (6 g) kelp powder (see Hot Tips on page 46)

Vegetable oil, as needed

CHIPS

4 large russet potatoes

2 tbsp (30 ml) olive oil

1 tsp salt

¼ tsp black pepper

Slice the tofu twice down the middle lengthwise to make 3 large pieces. Slices those 3 pieces widthwise to create 6 rectangles.

In a large bowl, whisk together the milk, lemon juice, salt, black pepper and cayenne pepper.

Add the tofu to the bowl, pressing the tofu down into the milk mixture. Let the tofu marinate while you make the chips. Toss the tofu frequently to make sure it is marinating evenly.

To make the chips, preheat the oven to 450°F (232°C).

Wash the potatoes and cut them into small wedges. Arrange the potatoes in a single layer on a medium baking sheet. Drizzle the potatoes with the olive oil and sprinkle them with the salt and black pepper. Toss to coat.

Bake the potatoes for 15 minutes, flip them and bake for another 10 minutes, or until the potatoes are all golden brown.

Once the tofu has been marinating for at least 20 minutes, combine the cornmeal, flour, Old Bay Seasoning and kelp powder in a large zip-top bag. Shake to mix the ingredients together.

In a large skillet over high heat, bring 1 inch (2.5 cm) of the vegetable oil to 350°F (177°C).

(Continued)

Southern Faux Fish and Chips (Continued)

WHITE BARBECUE SAUCE

1 cup (220 g) vegan mayo

2 tbsp (30 ml) apple cider vinegar

2 tbsp (30 ml) water

1 tsp prepared vegan horseradish

1 tsp Dijon mustard

1 tsp agave syrup

½ tsp salt

½ tsp black pepper

1 tsp garlic powder

Remove a piece of tofu from the marinade, making sure it is wet all over. Score the top of the tofu with a knife in a crosshatch pattern. Be sure to make very shallow scores; if you stick the knife in too deep, the tofu will fall apart.

Add the scored tofu to the cornmeal mixture, seal the bag and toss it to fully coat the tofu. Place the coated tofu on a plate. Repeat this process with the remainder of the tofu.

Add 2 or 3 pieces of tofu to the oil and fry them on each side for 2 to 3 minutes, or until the tofu is golden brown and crispy.

Transfer the fried tofu pieces to a paper towel and sprinkle them with more salt and Old Bay Seasoning. Repeat this process with the remainder of the crusted tofu.

To make the white barbecue sauce, whisk together the mayo, vinegar, water, horseradish, mustard, agave syrup, salt, black pepper and garlic powder in a small bowl. Taste and adjust the seasonings.

Serve the faux fish and chips with the white barbecue sauce on the side.

Hot Tips: If you have a hard time finding kelp powder, you can use about ¼ cup (60 g) of finely chopped nori sheets.

If you would prefer to oven-fry the tofu, preheat the oven to 450°F (232°C). Spray a medium baking sheet with nonstick cooking spray. Place the tofu on the prepared baking sheet and spray the tofu with nonstick cooking spray. Bake the tofu for 15 minutes, flip it and bake another 10 to 15 minutes, until the tofu is brown and crunchy.

CAJUN *Brussels Sprouts* WITH CHEESY GRITS

Brussels sprouts are such an underrated vegetable. If made right, they are incredible. If tossed in Cajun spice and served with cheesy grits and a spicy maple drizzle, they are beyond incredible. If you are a Brussels sprouts skeptic, this is where that ends. It certainly doesn't hurt that they are piled on top of the most wonderfully cheesy, creamy grits ever, which are made possible with the help of vegan milk, vegan butter and nutritional yeast.

Serves: 2 to 4

CAJUN BRUSSELS SPROUTS

1 lb (450 g) fresh Brussels sprouts

2 tbsp (30 ml) olive oil

2 tsp (6 g) smoked paprika

1 tsp salt

1 tsp garlic powder

1 tsp onion powder

1 tsp dried oregano

½ tsp black pepper

½ tsp dried thyme

¼–½ tsp cayenne pepper

CHEESY GRITS

2 cups (480 ml) water

1¼ cups (300 ml) almond milk or other nondairy milk

¼ cup (15 g) nutritional yeast

1 tsp salt

1 cup (170 g) yellow or white grits (see Hot Tip on page 49)

¼ cup (60 g) vegan butter

To make the Brussels sprouts, preheat the oven to 375°F (191°C). Spray a medium baking sheet with nonstick spray.

Trim the Brussels sprouts, cutting off the stems and removing any loose leaves.

Transfer the Brussels sprouts to a medium bowl, then drizzle them with the oil. Toss to coat.

In a small bowl, combine the smoked paprika, salt, garlic powder, onion powder, oregano, black pepper, thyme and cayenne pepper (use ¼ teaspoon of cayenne pepper if you prefer mild food or ½ teaspoon if you like more spice). Stir to combine the spices. Sprinkle the spices over the Brussels sprouts and toss to coat them completely.

Arrange the Brussels sprouts in a single layer on the prepared baking sheet. Bake for 20 to 25 minutes, or until the Brussels sprouts are soft (but not mushy) and brown.

While the Brussels sprouts are baking, make the cheesy grits. In a medium saucepan over medium-high heat, combine the water, milk, nutritional yeast and salt. Stir to combine the ingredients, then bring them to a boil.

(Continued)

Cajun Brussels Sprouts with Cheesy Grits (Continued)

SPICY MAPLE DRIZZLE

2 tbsp (30 ml) pure maple syrup

½ tsp hot sauce

Reduce the heat to medium-low and very slowly add the grits, whisking constantly. The more slowly you add the grits, the less likely they will be to form lumps.

Reduce the heat to low. Cover the saucepan and cook for 10 to 15 minutes, stirring frequently, until the grits are thick and soft.

Turn off the heat, then add the butter. Let it melt slightly, then stir it into the grits. Taste and adjust the seasoning.

When the Brussels sprouts and cheesy grits are done, make the spicy maple drizzle. In a small bowl, whisk together the maple syrup and hot sauce.

To serve, place some of the cheesy grits in a bowl. Top them with some of the Brussels sprouts and dress the Brussels sprouts with the spicy maple drizzle.

Hot Tip: If you can't find a package that is labeled specifically as grits, yellow or white cornmeal will also work.

Blackened Tofu and Coleslaw *Sandwiches*

Ah, sandwiches. I'll enjoy pretty much any sandwich you put in front of me and smile happily as I polish it off. However, there are "I enjoyed that" sandwiches and there are "Knock me on the floor, I think I will be marrying this sandwich" kind of sandwiches. These Blackened Tofu and Coleslaw Sandwiches are the latter. After tasting the spicy, crispy tofu and tangy, creamy coleslaw on toasted, crusty bread, you'll want to propose immediately.

Serves: 4

Blackened Tofu

1 (15-oz [450-g]) block extra-firm tofu, pressed (see page 37)

1 tbsp (15 ml) olive oil

2 tsp (10 g) Dijon mustard

2 tsp (6 g) smoked paprika

1 tsp salt

½ tsp ground cumin

½ tsp black pepper

½ tsp dried thyme

Pinch of cayenne pepper, or to taste

Coleslaw

2 tbsp (28 g) vegan mayo

1 tsp apple cider vinegar

1 tsp Dijon mustard

1 tsp agave syrup

Salt, to taste

Black pepper, to taste

2 cups (680 g) shredded cabbage

½ cup (25 g) shredded carrots

Sandwiches

4 vegan ciabatta or sourdough rolls

Vegan mayo, as needed

To make the blackened tofu, preheat the oven to 375°F (191°C). Spray a medium baking sheet with nonstick spray.

Slice the tofu into thin rectangles about ½ inch (13 mm) thick. Place the tofu slices in a large bowl and add the oil and mustard. Using your hands, toss the tofu and rub each slice with the oil and mustard, coating the tofu completely.

In a small bowl, combine the paprika, salt, cumin, black pepper, thyme and cayenne pepper.

Sprinkle the seasoning mixture over the tofu and toss with your hands again. Rub the seasoning evenly over all the tofu.

Lay each slice of tofu on the prepared baking sheet. Bake the tofu for 15 minutes, flip each slice and bake for 10 to 15 minutes more, or until the tofu is brown and firm and the seasoning is dark.

While the tofu is baking, make the coleslaw. In a large bowl, whisk together the mayo, vinegar, mustard, agave syrup, salt and black pepper.

Add the shredded cabbage and carrots to the bowl and toss to coat them in the dressing. Taste and adjust the seasonings.

When the tofu is done, make the sandwiches. Toast the rolls if desired. Then spread the mayo on both sides of the rolls. Top the bottoms of the rolls with the coleslaw and a few slices of blackened tofu, then place the top rolls on top of the tofu.

NASHVILLE HOT *Cauliflower*

No animals were harmed in the making of this Nashville hot chicken–inspired recipe. These little bites of juicy cauliflower are a perfect replacement for poultry. They are so dang crispy and crunchy that thinking about them keeps me up at night. The Nashville hot sauce these golden nuggets are tossed in tastes like nothing else, and no one should have to live without this recipe.

Serves: 4

CAULIFLOWER

1 medium head cauliflower

2 cups (480 ml) soy milk or other nondairy milk

2 tsp (10 ml) apple cider vinegar

2 tsp (10 ml) hot sauce

2 cups (240 g) all-purpose flour

1 tsp salt

2½ cups (140 g) panko breadcrumbs

Scallions, for topping

SAUCE

½ cup (120 g) vegan butter

¼ cup (60 ml) olive oil

3 tbsp (45 ml) hot sauce

¼ cup (60 ml) agave syrup

1½ tsp (5 g) smoked paprika

1 tsp garlic powder

1 tsp salt

To make the cauliflower, preheat the oven to 375°F (191°C). Spray a medium baking sheet with nonstick spray.

Cut the cauliflower into 1-inch (2.5-cm) florets and set them aside.

Set 3 medium bowls in a row to form a dredging station. In the first bowl, whisk together the milk, vinegar and hot sauce. In the second bowl, whisk together the flour and salt. Add the breadcrumbs to the third bowl.

Dip a cauliflower floret in the milk mixture then put it in the flour, coating it completely. Dip it in the milk mixture again, then back in the flour, dip it in the milk mixture a third time, then coat it completely in the breadcrumbs. Place the floret on the prepared baking sheet.

Repeat the preceding steps with all of the cauliflower florets. (I like to dredge 3 or 4 florets at a time to speed up the process.)

Spray the cauliflower with nonstick spray and bake for 10 minutes. Flip the cauliflower and bake for 15 to 20 minutes more, or until it is brown and crispy.

After flipping the cauliflower, make the sauce. In a medium saucepan over medium-low heat, combine the butter, oil, hot sauce, agave syrup, smoked paprika, garlic powder and salt. Heat the mixture, whisking to combine, until the butter has melted and all the ingredients are fully incorporated, 2 to 3 minutes. Remove the saucepan from the heat.

When the cauliflower is done, transfer it to a large bowl and pour the sauce on top. Toss to coat all the cauliflower in the sauce. Top with scallions.

Serve the cauliflower with pickles or Quick Spicy Pickled Green Beans (page 117). Add extra sauce for dipping.

GARLIC AND WILD MUSHROOM *Pot Roast*

When I stopped eating meat, it hit me like a ton of bricks: No more pot roast (cue my sad face). This vegan pot roast makes up for every night spent lying awake, staring at the ceiling and wondering how I'd survive. In fact, it makes up for everything bad that's ever happened to me. With loads of aromatic garlic, satiating mushrooms and rich red wine, this simple yet beautiful meal is hearty and comforting. Serve it over some Creamy Garlic-Truffle Grits (page 102) and wonderful things will happen.

Serves: 6

3 tbsp (45 ml) olive oil

6 cloves garlic, coarsely chopped

1 lb (450 g) Yukon gold potatoes, diced

4 large carrots, coarsely chopped

½ medium sweet onion, coarsely chopped

Salt, to taste

Black pepper, to taste

10 oz (300 g) cremini mushrooms, coarsely chopped

6 oz (180 g) portobello mushrooms, coarsely chopped

4 oz (120 g) shiitake mushrooms, coarsely chopped

4 oz (120 g) oyster mushrooms, coarsely chopped

1 cup (240 ml) vegan sweet red wine

2 cups (480 ml) vegetable broth

3 sprigs fresh rosemary

2 sprigs fresh thyme

In a large, oven-safe pot, heat the oil over medium-high heat.

Add the garlic, potatoes, carrots and onion. Sauté, reducing the heat as needed to prevent burning, for 8 to 10 minutes, or until the potatoes and carrots are beginning to soften and the onion is translucent. Season the vegetables with a pinch of salt and black pepper.

Preheat the oven to 350°F (177°C).

Add the cremini mushrooms, portobello mushrooms, shiitake mushrooms and oyster mushrooms to the pot. Toss to combine everything, season the mixture with a pinch of salt and black pepper and sauté until the mushrooms have released their liquid and are beginning to brown, 5 to 10 minutes.

Add the wine, stir and scrape the bottom of the pot to loosen any bits that are stuck to the bottom. Add the broth, rosemary and thyme. Stir to combine. Season with a pinch of salt and black pepper. Bring the mixture to a simmer over medium-high heat then reduce to medium-low.

Cover the pot and roast the vegetables for 20 to 25 minutes, or until the potatoes and carrots are soft.

Remove the pot from the oven. Remove and discard the rosemary and thyme sprigs. Serve the pot roast with mashed potatoes, noodles, grits, cauliflower mash or any starch you want.

COWBOY *Chili*

I do not take this next sentence lightly: This chili is unrivaled. The coffee makes it unique and gives it an incredible richness. It's a fast meal that will fill you up and warm you to your core. This chili will be on heavy rotation when the weather starts to get cool.

Serves: 4 to 6

1 tbsp (15 ml) olive oil

½ medium sweet onion, diced

6 cloves garlic, finely chopped

2 (15-oz [450-g]) cans black beans, drained and rinsed

2 (15-oz [450-g]) cans kidney beans, drained and rinsed

2 tbsp (18 g) chili powder

2 tsp (4 g) instant coffee powder

2 tsp (6 g) ground cumin

1 tsp smoked paprika

1 tbsp (15 ml) coconut aminos or soy sauce

2 tbsp (30 g) tomato paste

Salt, to taste

Black pepper, to taste

3 cups (720 ml) vegetable broth

⅓ cup (45 g) pickled jalapeños, diced

Minced fresh cilantro (optional)

Vegan sour cream (optional)

Vegan corn chips (optional)

Heat the oil in a large pot over medium-high heat. Add the onion and garlic and sauté, reducing the heat as needed to prevent burning, until the onion is translucent, 3 to 5 minutes.

Add the black beans, kidney beans, chili powder, coffee powder, cumin, smoked paprika, coconut aminos, tomato paste and a few pinches of salt and black pepper.

Stir to fully combine the ingredients, reduce the heat to low and sauté for 2 to 3 minutes.

Add the broth and bring the chili to a simmer. Cook for 15 to 20 minutes to develop the flavor and allow the chili to thicken.

Add the jalapeños and a few more pinches of salt and black pepper. Stir to combine and simmer for 2 to 3 minutes. Taste and adjust the seasonings, adding more salt and black pepper if needed.

Serve the chili topped with the cilantro (if using), sour cream (if using) and corn chips (if using).

Carolina Barbecue Seitan *Wings*

Of all the recipes I've developed, these seitan wings are my husband's favorite. This is the easiest seitan recipe in the world, and every time my husband realizes what I am making, he turns giddy. Tossed in my version of the classic, mustard-heavy barbecue sauce from South Carolina, these seitan wings will melt in your mouth.

Serves: 6

Seitan Wings

2 cups (288 g) vital wheat gluten

1 tsp garlic powder

1½ tsp (8 g) salt

1¼ cups (300 ml) vegetable broth

1 tbsp (15 ml) olive oil

Finely chopped fresh chives (optional)

Mustard Barbecue Sauce

1 cup (240 ml) tomato sauce

3 tbsp (45 ml) apple cider vinegar

¼ cup (60 ml) pure maple syrup

¼ cup (64 g) Dijon mustard

1 tbsp (9 g) vegan brown sugar

1 tsp onion powder

1 tsp garlic powder

Pinch of salt

Pinch of cayenne pepper

To make the seitan wings, stir together the vital wheat gluten, garlic powder and salt in a large bowl.

Slowly stir in the broth, and when the gluten becomes too hard to stir, knead it with your hands until the seitan comes together and forms a ball.

Bring a large pot of salted water to a boil over high heat. Pull tiny pieces of seitan from the dough ball and drop them in the water. Continue this process until all the dough is used. (The seitan will expand; the smaller the pieces you pull off, the better.)

Boil the seitan, reducing the heat if needed, for 30 minutes. Drain the pot and let the seitan cool completely.

While the seitan cools, preheat the oven to 375°F (191°C).

When the seitan pieces are cool enough to handle, squeeze as much liquid out of them as possible with your hands. Place the wings on a medium baking sheet. Drizzle the oil onto the wings and toss to coat them.

Bake the wings for 20 minutes, flip them and bake for 20 to 25 minutes more, or until they are brown and firm.

When the wings are almost done, make the barbecue sauce. In a small saucepan over medium-low heat, whisk together the tomato sauce, vinegar, maple syrup, mustard, brown sugar, onion powder, garlic powder, salt and cayenne pepper. Bring the sauce to a simmer, reduce the heat to low and simmer for 10 to 15 minutes. Taste and adjust the seasonings. Remove the saucepan from the heat

When the wings are done, toss them in the barbecue sauce and serve them topped with the chives (if using).

Gettin' Fancy for SUPPER TIME

Put on your bow ties and little black dresses, because the recipes you will find in this chapter are dressed to impress. These delightfully fancy meals may be a little more time consuming, but they are worth the wait. The amazing dishes in this chapter leave their mark on anyone who tries them. Meat eaters will be begging for more and asking you where you got the recipe.

These are the Sunday suppers you've been dreaming of. You'll probably want to make these dinners for all the naysayers in your life, the ones who think vegans eat only salad. Invite your whole family over and show off your mad cooking skills! Place one of these fancy suppers, like the Fancy-Schmancy Meatloaf with Garlic Cauliflower Mash (page 69), in front of anyone at any time and watch as you blow their mind.

CHEESY BISCUIT VEGETABLE *Pot Pie*

Hot, fluffy, flaky, cheesy biscuits baked on top of a creamy vegetable pie filling—this is not a drill, people. I've made this pot pie just for you, and it's spectacular. This pot pie will feed a crowd, so gather your favorite people and dig in!

Serves: 6 to 8

POT PIE FILLING

⅓ cup (80 g) vegan butter

⅓ cup (40 g) all-purpose flour

1 cup (240 ml) vegetable broth

3 cups (720 ml) nondairy milk

2 tsp (10 g) Dijon mustard

Salt, to taste

Black pepper, to taste

8 oz (240 g) baby potatoes, cut in half

1 tbsp (15 ml) olive oil

3 medium carrots, diced

4 cloves garlic, finely chopped

2 cups (300 g) frozen green beans

1 (15-oz [450-g]) can corn, drained

1 tsp poultry seasoning

To make the pot pie filling, melt the butter in a large pot over medium heat. When the butter has melted, add the flour and whisk to make a roux.

Cook the roux for 1 minute, then add the broth, milk and mustard. Whisk to combine, making sure there are no lumps. Season with a pinch of salt and black pepper.

Bring the mixture to a simmer, then add the potatoes. Simmer for about 15 minutes, stirring frequently or until the sauce has thickened and the potatoes are tender.

In the meantime, heat the oil in a large nonstick skillet over medium-high heat. Add the carrots and garlic and sauté for about 5 minutes, until the garlic is golden brown. Add the green beans and sauté for about 5 minutes, until the carrots and green beans are soft. Season with a pinch of salt and black pepper.

When the potatoes are tender and the carrots and green beans are cooked, transfer the carrots and green beans to the pot with the potatoes and cream sauce. Add the corn and poultry seasoning to the filling. Stir to combine, then simmer for 2 minutes, or until the filling is thick. Taste and adjust the seasonings.

Pour the pot pie filling into a 9 x 9–inch (23 x 23–cm) baking dish. Set the filling aside.

(Continued)

Cheesy Biscuit Vegetable Pot Pie (Continued)

CHEESY BISCUITS

2 cups (240 g) all-purpose flour

2 tsp (8 g) baking powder

½ tsp baking soda

1 tsp salt

¼ cup (15 g) nutritional yeast

¾ cup (180 ml) nondairy milk

1 tsp distilled white vinegar

⅓ cup (80 g) cold vegan butter

Olive oil, as needed

Minced fresh thyme, rosemary or parsley (optional)

Preheat the oven to 400°F (204°C).

To make the cheesy biscuits, sift the flour, baking powder and baking soda into a large bowl. Stir in the salt and nutritional yeast.

In a small bowl, mix together the milk and vinegar and set the mixture aside for 1 minute to allow the milk to thicken.

Break the butter up into small pieces with your fingers and drop them into the flour mixture. Press and pinch the butter into the flour using your fingers or a fork until the butter is evenly distributed and the flour resembles sand.

Add the milk mixture to the flour mixture and stir to combine. Once it becomes too difficult to stir, knead the dough with your hands for about 1 minute to form a ball.

Put the dough on a floured surface. Pat out the dough and fold it over, then roll the dough out until it is about ½ inch (13 mm) thick. Cut 9 to 10 small biscuits out of the dough. Use all the dough to make biscuits by bringing the dough scraps together into a ball and rolling it out again. Place the biscuits on top of the pot pie filling.

Brush the tops of the biscuits with the oil and bake the pot pie for 15 to 20 minutes, or until the biscuits are golden brown and cooked through. Serve big scoops of the pot pie in individual bowls and sprinkled with the fresh herbs (if using).

BARBECUE TEMPEH AND SWEET *Corn Pudding*

In the summer, I crave barbecue paired with any kind of corn. The combination in this recipe is an absolute gem. Dry-rubbed tempeh that is baked and then brushed with barbecue sauce is sweet corn pudding's long-lost best friend! Every component of this recipe will class-up your family get-togethers or summer holiday dinners and wow your guests!

Serves: 4

BARBECUE TEMPEH

1 lb (450 g) tempeh

¼ cup (60 ml) soy sauce or coconut aminos

¼ cup (60 ml) water

2 tbsp (30 ml) pure maple syrup

2 tsp (6 g) smoked paprika

2 tsp (6 g) garlic powder

1 tsp onion powder

1 tsp chili powder

2 tsp (6 g) vegan brown sugar

1 tsp salt

1 batch Mustard Barbecue Sauce (page 58) or 1 cup (240 ml) store-bought vegan barbecue sauce, plus more as needed

Chives, for topping

SWEET CORN PUDDING

4 cups (700 g) fresh or canned corn (drained if canned)

⅓ cup (64 g) vegan granulated sugar

1 tsp salt

1 cup (240 ml) full-fat coconut milk or coconut cream

½ cup (60 g) all-purpose flour

½ cup (85 g) cornmeal

2 tbsp (18 g) cornstarch

1 tsp baking powder

Preheat the oven to 350°F (177°C). Spray a medium baking sheet with nonstick cooking spray. Spray a 9 x 9–inch (23 x 23–cm) baking dish with nonstick cooking spray.

To make the barbecue tempeh, cut the tempeh into 1-inch (2.5-cm)-thick strips. Set the tempeh aside.

In a large bowl, whisk together the soy sauce, water and maple syrup. Add the tempeh to the soy sauce mixture and toss to coat it. Let the tempeh marinate while you make the corn pudding.

To make the sweet corn pudding, stir together the corn, granulated sugar, salt and coconut milk in a large bowl.

In a medium bowl, stir together the flour, cornmeal, cornstarch and baking powder.

(Continued)

Barbecue Tempeh and
Sweet Corn Pudding (Continued)

Add the flour mixture to the corn mixture and stir to combine.

Pour the corn pudding into the prepared baking dish. Spread the pudding out evenly in the dish. Set the corn pudding aside.

Check on the tempeh. If there is a lot of excess marinade in the bowl, drain it, but make sure the tempeh is wet.

In a small bowl, stir together the smoked paprika, garlic powder, onion powder, chili powder, brown sugar and salt.

Sprinkle the seasoning mixture over the tempeh and rub the seasoning onto all sides of the tempeh, coating each piece thoroughly. Transfer the seasoned tempeh to the prepared baking sheet.

Place the corn pudding and tempeh into the oven at the same time. Bake the corn pudding for 30 to 40 minutes, or until it is golden brown. Bake the tempeh for 15 minutes, remove it from the oven and brush the top of the tempeh with the Mustard Barbecue Sauce. Bake the tempeh for 10 minutes, flip it, brush the other side with the sauce and bake it for another 10 minutes.

The tempeh and corn pudding should be done at about the same time. Top with chives. Serve the tempeh with extra Mustard Barbecue Sauce and Quick Spicy Pickled Green Beans (page 117).

FANCY-SCHMANCY *Meatloaf* WITH GARLIC CAULIFLOWER MASH

Put on your top hat or tiara, because this meatloaf is fancy. It's moist but firm and completely irresistible. Serving it with a fluffy, creamy, luxurious garlic cauliflower mash is not just fancy—it's brilliant.

Serves: 4 to 6

MEATLOAF

1 tbsp (15 ml) olive oil

4 cloves garlic, finely chopped

½ medium sweet onion, diced

1 large carrot, diced

10 oz (300 g) cremini mushrooms, diced

Pinch plus 1 tsp salt, divided

Pinch plus ½ tsp black pepper, divided

3 cups (225 g) cooked brown lentils

1 cup (55 g) panko breadcrumbs

¼ cup (60 g) ketchup

1 tbsp (15 ml) liquid aminos or soy sauce

1 tbsp (15 ml) molasses

½ cup (120 ml) Mustard Barbecue Sauce (page 58) or store-bought vegan barbecue sauce, divided

To make the meatloaf, preheat the oven to 375°F (191°C). Spray a 9 x 5–inch (23 x 13–cm) loaf pan with nonstick cooking spray. Heat the oil in a large nonstick skillet over medium-high heat. Add the garlic, onion, carrot and mushrooms. Season with the pinch of salt and the pinch of black pepper. Sauté, reducing the heat as needed to prevent burning, for 4 to 5 minutes, or until the onion is translucent and the mushrooms are brown. Remove the skillet from the heat and set it aside.

In a large bowl, mash the lentils with a fork. Make sure to smash them as much as you can while leaving a bit of texture.

Add the sautéed vegetables, breadcrumbs, ketchup, liquid aminos, molasses, the remaining 1 teaspoon of salt and the remaining ½ teaspoon of black pepper to the lentils. Stir to combine, then fold the mixture together with your hands until you can form a ball.

Press the lentil mixture into the prepared loaf pan.

Pour ¼ cup (60 ml) of the Mustard Barbecue Sauce on top of the loaf and spread it out evenly.

(Continued)

GARLIC CAULIFLOWER MASH

1 large head cauliflower, cut into 1-inch (2.5-cm) florets

4 cloves garlic

⅓ cup (80 ml) nondairy milk

2 tbsp (30 g) vegan butter

1 tsp salt

½ tsp black pepper

Red Wine–Shallot Gravy (page 76; optional)

Bake the meatloaf for 30 minutes. Brush the top of the loaf with the remaining ¼ cup (60 ml) of Mustard Barbecue Sauce. Bake for another 10 minutes, or until the loaf is very firm and brown.

While the meatloaf is baking, make the garlic cauliflower mash.

Bring a large pot of salted water to a boil over high heat. Add the cauliflower and garlic to the water. Boil for 8 to 10 minutes, or until the cauliflower is tender. Drain the pot and transfer the cauliflower and garlic to a blender.

Add the milk, butter, salt and black pepper to the blender. Pulse until the cauliflower is smooth. Taste and adjust the seasonings.

Serve the meatloaf and mash with the Red Wine–Shallot Gravy (if using) drizzled on top.

PEPPERY BARBECUE *Hand Pies*

Barbecue pulled jackfruit inside a buttery, peppery crust: Your world is about to change in the most delightful way. Savory hand pies are where it's at! I love to serve them with my White Barbecue Sauce (page 46).

Serves: 4

½ cup (120 ml) plus 2 tbsp (30 ml) Mustard Barbecue Sauce (page 58) or store-bought vegan barbecue sauce, divided

½ cup (120 ml) vegetable broth

1 (20-oz [600-g]) can young green jackfruit in water, drained

Pinch plus 1 tsp salt, divided

Pinch plus 2 tsp (4 g) black pepper, divided

2½ cups (300 g) all-purpose flour

¾ cup (180 g) cold vegan butter

½ cup (120 ml) ice-cold water

Olive oil, as needed

White Barbecue Sauce (page 46)

In a large nonstick skillet, whisk together ½ cup (120 ml) of the Mustard Barbecue Sauce and the broth. Add the jackfruit.

Bring the jackfruit to a simmer over medium-high heat and cook for about 5 minutes, or until it starts to get tender and you can start to smash the jackfruit with a fork. Smash it as much as possible.

Continue to simmer the jackfruit, reducing the heat if needed to prevent burning, for about 10 minutes, or until the jackfruit is tender enough to smash and shred completely and the sauce has been absorbed.

Season the jackfruit with the pinch of salt and pinch of black pepper. Remove the jackfruit from the heat.

Stir the remaining 2 tablespoons (30 ml) of Mustard Barbecue Sauce into the jackfruit to coat all of it. Set it aside to cool.

Sift the flour into a large bowl, then stir in the remaining 1 teaspoon of salt and 2 teaspoons (4 g) of black pepper.

Break the butter up into small pieces and drop them into the flour. Using your hands or a fork, press the butter into the flour until it is evenly distributed and the flour resembles sand.

Pour the water into the flour a little at a time, stirring until it gets too hard to stir. Knead with your hands for about 1 minute until the dough forms a ball.

Put the dough in the fridge to chill for about 5 minutes.

(Continued)

Peppery Barbecue Hand Pies (Continued)

Preheat the oven to 450°F (232°C). Spray a medium baking sheet with nonstick cooking spray.

Transfer the dough to a floured work surface. Roll the dough out until it is about ⅛ inch (3 mm) thick (see Hot Tip). Cut the dough into 3-inch (7.5-cm) circles.

Put 1 to 2 tablespoons (9 to 18 g) of the jackfruit in the center of one circle of dough, then top the jackfruit with another circle. Press a fork around the edges of the dough to seal the hand pie.

Repeat the preceding process with all the dough and jackfruit. Poke a few holes in the tops of the hand pies and brush the tops lightly with the oil. Place the hand pies on the prepared baking sheet.

Bake the hand pies for 15 to 18 minutes, or until they are golden brown and crisp.

Serve the hand pies with the White Barbecue Sauce or extra Mustard Barbecue Sauce.

Hot Tip: If you find it difficult to visually measure the thickness of the dough, try stacking two US quarters on top of each other—two stacked quarters are roughly ⅛ inch (3 mm) in height.

ROASTED ROOT *Vegetables* WITH MASHED POTATOES AND RED WINE—SHALLOT GRAVY

Mercy me, this entire situation is delicious. I can't think of a better way to eat my veggies. Roasted until brown and juicy, piled on top of the most luscious mashed potatoes and covered in a uniquely wonderful gravy.

Serves: 4 to 6

ROASTED ROOT VEGETABLES

2 cups (256 g) coarsely chopped carrots

2 cups (266 g) diced sweet potatoes

1 cup (128 g) coarsely chopped parsnips

10 large cloves garlic

½ medium Vidalia onion, diced

2 tbsp (30 ml) olive oil

1 tsp dried thyme

1 tsp salt

½ tsp black pepper

MASHED POTATOES

3 lbs (1.4 kg) russet potatoes, peeled and diced

½ cup (120 g) vegan butter

½ cup (120 ml) nondairy milk

½ cup (120 ml) full-fat coconut milk or coconut cream

Salt, to taste

Black pepper, to taste

Preheat the oven to 375°F (191°C).

Put the carrots, sweet potatoes, parsnips, garlic and onion on a medium baking sheet.

Drizzle the oil over the vegetables and then sprinkle them with the thyme, salt and black pepper. Toss to coat all the vegetables.

Roast the vegetables for 20 to 25 minutes, or until they are brown and cooked through.

In the meantime, make the mashed potatoes. Add the potatoes to a large pot of cold water. Bring the water to a boil over high heat, then reduce the heat to medium. Simmer the potatoes for 15 to 20 minutes, or until they are very tender.

(Continued)

RED WINE–SHALLOT GRAVY

½ cup (120 g) vegan butter

2 medium shallots, diced

¼ cup (30 g) all-purpose flour

2½ cups (600 ml) vegetable broth

¼ cup (60 ml) vegan red wine

1 tbsp (15 ml) balsamic vinegar

2 sprigs fresh thyme

Salt, to taste

Black pepper, to taste

While the vegetables are roasting and the potatoes are boiling, start the red wine–shallot gravy.

In a large nonstick skillet over medium-high heat, melt the butter. Add the shallots.

Sauté the shallots, reducing the heat as needed to prevent burning, for 3 to 5 minutes, or until the shallots are translucent.

Add the flour and stir to coat the shallots in the flour. Add the broth, wine (I like to use cabernet sauvignon) and vinegar and whisk to combine. Make sure there are no lumps of flour.

Add the thyme and a few pinches of salt and black pepper.

Simmer the gravy for 10 to 15 minutes, or until it is thick and the strong red wine flavor has cooked off. Taste and adjust the seasonings. Keep the gravy warm.

When the potatoes are tender, drain them and return them to the pot. Mash all of the potatoes with a potato masher.

Add the butter, nondairy milk, coconut milk, salt and black pepper. Mash the ingredients together and then stir until the potatoes are creamy. Taste and adjust the seasonings.

To serve, put some mashed potatoes in a bowl, top them with some roasted vegetables and drizzle everything with some gravy.

DELUXE SOUTHERN *Reuben*

What makes this dish fancy, you ask? It's dressed up for a night out! Marble rye bread gets slathered with a rich Mississippi Comeback Sauce and topped with zesty Pickled Collard Greens and corned tempeh. Yup, it's as amazing as it sounds.

Serves: 3 to 4

CORNED TEMPEH

8 oz (240 g) tempeh, thinly sliced

1 cup (240 ml) water

1 tsp salt

1 tsp vegan granulated sugar

1 tsp pickling spice

1 tsp ground coriander

½ tsp vegan brown sugar

¼ tsp mustard seeds

¼ tsp black pepper

PICKLED COLLARD GREENS

8 oz (240 g) coarsely chopped destemmed collard greens

¼ cup (60 ml) distilled white vinegar

¼ cup (60 ml) apple cider vinegar

2 tbsp (30 ml) water

1 tsp salt

1 tsp vegan granulated sugar

4 cloves garlic, smashed

Pinch of cayenne pepper

To make the corned tempeh, put the sliced tempeh into a large heatproof bowl. Set the bowl aside.

In a small saucepan over medium-high heat, combine the water, salt, granulated sugar, pickling spice, coriander, brown sugar, mustard seeds and black pepper.

Bring the mixture to a simmer, then turn off the heat. Stir the mixture to make sure the sugars and salt have dissolved.

Pour the liquid over the tempeh, making sure the tempeh is submerged in the liquid. Let the tempeh marinate for at least 1 hour.

While the tempeh is marinating, make the pickled collard greens.

Bring a large pot of salted water to a boil over high heat. Add the collard greens and reduce the heat to low. Simmer the greens for about 10 minutes, or until they are tender. Drain the greens and put them in another large heatproof bowl.

In a small saucepan over medium heat, combine the distilled white vinegar, apple cider vinegar, water, salt, granulated sugar, garlic and cayenne pepper. Bring the mixture to a simmer, then remove it from the heat and pour the liquid over the collard greens. Set the collard greens aside to marinate while you finish preparing the recipe.

(Continued)

Deluxe Southern Reuben (Continued)

MISSISSIPPI COMEBACK SAUCE

1 cup (220 g) vegan mayo

2 tbsp (30 ml) hot sauce

¼ cup (60 g) ketchup

2 tsp (10 ml) liquid aminos or soy sauce

1 clove garlic, finely chopped

1 tsp garlic powder

1 tsp onion powder

½ tsp smoked paprika

SANDWICHES

6–8 slices vegan marble rye bread

Preheat the oven to 400°F (204°C). Spray a medium baking sheet with nonstick cooking spray.

Remove the tempeh from the marinade. Place the tempeh on the prepared baking sheet. Bake the tempeh for 15 minutes, flip it and bake for 10 to 15 minutes more, or until it is brown.

While the tempeh bakes, make the Mississippi Comeback Sauce.

In a small bowl, whisk together the mayo, hot sauce, ketchup, liquid aminos, garlic, garlic powder, onion powder and smoked paprika.

To assemble the sandwiches, spread the Mississippi Comeback Sauce on a slice of marble rye bread. Take some of the pickled collard greens out of the pickling liquid and squeeze some of the liquid out. Put the collards on the Mississippi Comeback Sauce, then place several pieces of tempeh on the collards. Put some Mississippi Comeback Sauce on the other slice of bread. Top the tempeh with the other slice of bread and serve.

SMOTHERED Steaks AND GREENS

Healthy, filling and downright stunning, these "hamburger steaks" are a simple mixture of lentils and quinoa. They are baked and smothered in the most wonderful gravy and greens. Serve these with any of your favorite sides, like some Sweet 'n' Spicy Cornbread (page 105)!

Serves: 4

1 cup (75 g) cooked brown lentils

½ cup (93 g) cooked quinoa

2 tbsp (14 g) flax meal

3 tbsp (45 ml) water

¾ cup (41 g) panko breadcrumbs

3 tbsp (45 ml) olive oil, divided

1 tsp liquid smoke

2 tsp (10 ml) soy sauce

1 tsp garlic powder

½ tsp salt, plus more as needed

¼ tsp black pepper, plus more as needed

½ medium sweet onion, thinly sliced

2 tbsp (16 g) all-purpose flour

1½ cups (360 ml) vegetable broth

2 cups (134 g) coarsely chopped kale

Preheat the oven to 375°F (191°C). Spray a medium baking sheet with nonstick cooking spray.

In a large bowl, mash the lentils with a fork. Make sure they are all mashed. Add the quinoa to the lentils and stir to combine.

In a small bowl, whisk together the flax meal and water. Let the mixture sit to thicken for 3 to 5 minutes.

Add the flax mixture, breadcrumbs, 1 tablespoon (15 ml) of the oil, liquid smoke, soy sauce, garlic powder, salt and black pepper to the lentils and quinoa. Stir to combine, then use your hands to form the mixture into a ball.

Divide the mixture into 4 portions. Roll each portion into a ball, pressing it together and then flattening it out into a "steak." Place the steaks on the prepared baking sheet. Bake the steaks for 15 minutes, flip them and bake for another 15 minutes, or until the steaks are firm.

While the steaks are baking, heat the remaining 2 tablespoons (30 ml) of oil in a large nonstick skillet over medium-high heat. Add the onion and sauté, reducing the heat as needed to prevent burning, for about 10 minutes, or until the onion is starting to brown. Season it with a pinch of salt and black pepper.

Add the flour to the onion and stir to coat the onion in the flour and make a paste. Pour in the broth and whisk to combine, making sure there are no lumps of flour. Reduce the heat to low. Simmer the gravy for 2 to 4 minutes, or until it has thickened.

Add the kale to the gravy and stir to combine. Cook the kale in the gravy for 2 to 4 minutes, or until the kale is tender.

Season the kale with a few pinches of salt and black pepper. Taste and adjust the seasonings. Turn off the heat.

Once the steaks are done, add them to the gravy. Spoon the gravy and greens on top of the steaks and serve.

Pecan-Crusted *Tofu* with Mashed Sweet Potatoes

Fall is my absolute favorite season, and nothing screams fall quite like pecan-crusted tofu served with maple-sweetened mashed sweet potatoes. It's the perfect holiday dinner party meal and the one I throw down when I want to impress.

Serves: 4

Mashed Sweet Potatoes

6 large sweet potatoes, peeled and diced

¾ cup (180 ml) nondairy milk

½ cup (60 g) vegan butter, plus more as needed

¼ cup (60 ml) pure maple syrup, plus more as needed (optional)

1 tbsp (9 g) vegan brown sugar

Salt, to taste

Pecan-Crusted Tofu

1 (15-oz [450-g]) block extra-firm tofu, pressed (see page 37)

½ cup (125 g) Dijon mustard

1 tbsp (15 ml) agave syrup

3 tbsp (45 ml) water

1½ cups (180 g) roasted pecans

1 cup (55 g) panko breadcrumbs

Salt, to taste

Dried thyme, for topping

To make the mashed sweet potatoes, bring a large pot of salted water to a boil over high heat. Add the sweet potatoes, reduce the heat to medium-low and simmer until the sweet potatoes can be smashed with a fork, about 25 minutes.

In the meantime, make the pecan-crusted tofu. Preheat the oven to 375°F (191°C). Spray a medium baking sheet with nonstick cooking spray.

Cut the tofu into 6 to 8 triangles or rectangles. Set them aside.

In a medium bowl, whisk together the Dijon, agave syrup and water. Set the bowl aside.

In a food processor, pulse the pecans until they are finely ground. (Don't overprocess the pecans or they will turn to pecan butter.) Transfer the pecans to another medium bowl.

Add the breadcrumbs to the pecans. Season the mixture with the salt, stirring to combine.

Dip each piece of tofu into the mustard mixture, coating it completely. Put the tofu in the bowl with the pecan mixture. Press the mixture onto the tofu and coat the entire piece. Place the tofu on the prepared baking sheet. Repeat this process with all of the tofu.

Bake the tofu for 10 minutes. Flip the tofu, then bake for another 10 minutes.

When the sweet potatoes are tender, drain them and return them to the pot. Mash the sweet potatoes, then add the nondairy milk, butter, maple syrup, brown sugar and salt. Whisk to combine, until the sweet potatoes are smooth. Taste and adjust the seasonings.

When the tofu is done, serve it on top of the sweet potatoes with a little butter and a drizzle of maple syrup if desired. Sprinkle with dried thyme.

Carbs Are
A SOUTHERN GAL'S
Best Friend

Be still my heart—a whole chapter dedicated to delicious carbs. I'm swooning.

Let me take you back to a world where all I ate was pasta tossed in olive oil and balsamic vinegar—a world of boring carbs, before I knew the possibilities. I was getting tired of the same old thing, and then I had an epiphany. I realized I could create my own recipes, keep my favorite southern flavors and make anything I wanted. So, say hello to your new best friends. The dishes in this chapter are what we all need in our lives: big ol' bowls of comfort, like the Collard Green Carbonara (page 92), tossed in the creamiest, dreamiest sauce. Or the Hoppin' John Risotto (page 91), which will ruin all other risottos for you. The pastas in this chapter are exciting, super easy, mouthwatering and anything but average!

SPICY SOUTHERN BROCCOLI *Fettuccine Alfredo*

I don't know what it is about the combination of this spicy broccoli and this perfectly creamy alfredo sauce, but it is beyond comparison. This healthy pasta dish is so dang comforting you would be hard-pressed to convince anyone it is simply roasted broccoli and pureed cashews.

Serves: 4

SPICY BROCCOLI

1 large head broccoli, cut into 1-inch (2.5-cm) florets

2 tbsp (30 ml) olive oil

1 tbsp (15 ml) agave syrup

1 tsp smoked paprika

1 tsp salt

½ tsp black pepper

½ tsp garlic powder

½ tsp onion powder

½ tsp cayenne pepper

FETTUCCINE ALFREDO

1 lb (450 g) fettuccine

1 cup (110 g) raw cashews, soaked (see Tips)

¾ cup (180 ml) nondairy milk

4 cloves garlic

2 tsp (10 ml) fresh lemon juice

3 tbsp (12 g) nutritional yeast

1 tsp salt

½ tsp black pepper

To make the spicy broccoli, preheat the oven to 375°F (191°C).

Put the broccoli florets in a large bowl, then drizzle them with the oil and agave syrup. Sprinkle the broccoli with the paprika, salt, black pepper, garlic powder, onion powder and cayenne pepper. Toss to coat the broccoli evenly.

Put the broccoli on a medium baking sheet and roast for 10 to 12 minutes, or until the broccoli is slightly brown.

In the meantime, make the fettuccini alfredo. Cook the fettuccine according to package directions. Drain the fettuccine and return it to the pot.

While the pasta cooks, drain the soaked cashews and add them to a blender with the milk, garlic, lemon juice, nutritional yeast, salt and black pepper.

Blend on high for 2 to 3 minutes, scraping down the sides of the blender as needed, until the sauce is completely smooth.

Pour the alfredo sauce on top of the pasta. Toss to combine the fettuccine with the sauce. Taste and adjust the seasonings.

Add the spicy broccoli to the pasta and serve.

Tips for Soaking Raw Cashews

There are two ways you can soak raw cashews. Choose the method that works best for you.

- Place the amount of raw cashews you need into a bowl. Cover them with cool or tepid water. Let them soak in the water for at least 6 hours. This is something you can prep in the morning or the night before.

- Place the amount of raw cashews you need in a heatproof bowl. In a small pot, bring enough water to cover the cashews to a boil over high heat. Pour the boiling water over the cashews and let them soak in the hot water for about 30 minutes.

ONE-POT VIDALIA ONION *Pasta*

Creamy, sweet and salty carbs, all in one pot? This is not a test; this is really happening. Caramelized Vidalia onions and garlic tossed with pasta that has been cooked in its own creamy sauce means you get maximum flavor with minimum effort. This is my go-to date night pasta. It is easy enough that you don't have to worry about messing it up and fancy enough to be romantic!

Serves: 4

2 tbsp (30 ml) olive oil

2 large Vidalia onions, thinly sliced

6 cloves garlic, finely chopped

1 tbsp (15 ml) agave syrup

Salt, to taste

Black pepper, to taste

1 tsp fresh lemon juice, plus more as needed

3 cups (720 ml) vegetable broth

2½ cups (600 ml) nondairy milk

2 sprigs fresh thyme

1 lb (450 g) cavatelli or other short pasta

Heat the oil in a large pot over medium heat.

Add the onions and garlic to the pot. Sauté, reducing the heat as needed to prevent burning, for about 10 minutes, or until the onions start to brown.

Add the agave syrup, salt and black pepper. Stir to coat the onions and garlic in the syrup.

Reduce the heat to medium-low and cook for about 15 minutes, or until the onions are totally brown and caramelized. Transfer the onions and garlic to a small bowl. Set the bowl aside.

Add the lemon juice to the pot and scrape any bits of onion and garlic from the bottom of the pot.

Add the broth and milk to the pot. Add the thyme and a pinch of salt and black pepper, stirring to combine.

Increase the heat to medium-high and bring the liquid to a boil.

Pour the pasta into the pot. Stir, then reduce the heat to medium. Cook the pasta for the amount of time listed on the package directions.

When the pasta is fully cooked, the liquid should be mostly absorbed and should be a thick sauce.

When the pasta is cooked, turn off the heat and season the pasta with salt and black pepper. Add the onions and garlic to the pasta. Toss to combine. Taste and adjust the seasonings. Serve immediately with extra lemon juice on top.

HOPPIN' JOHN *Risotto*

A traditional Hoppin' John dish includes black-eyed peas, rice and meat, and it sometimes includes bacon fat or ham hock. It's a common Low Country dish. However, this plant-based version gets real fancy! Nothing—seriously, nothing—is fancier than risotto. And my take on risotto is not only fancy but also flavorful and comforting.

Serves: 4

5 cups (1.2 L) vegetable broth

¼ cup (60 g) vegan butter

½ cup (75 g) diced sweet onion

6 cloves garlic, coarsely chopped

2 cups (420 g) arborio rice

1 cup (240 ml) vegan beer (preferably a pale ale)

1 tsp salt, plus more as needed

1 tsp dried thyme

1 tsp smoked paprika

Pinch of cayenne pepper

1 (15-oz [450-g]) can black-eyed peas, drained and rinsed

Black pepper, to taste

Finely chopped rosemary or chives, as needed

In a medium saucepan over medium-low heat, bring the broth to a simmer. Reduce the heat to low and keep the broth warm while you make the risotto.

In a large nonstick skillet over medium-high heat, melt the butter. Add the onion and garlic. Sauté, reducing the heat as needed to prevent burning, for 5 to 6 minutes, or until the onion is translucent and slightly brown.

Add the rice and toss it with the onion and garlic. Cook for about 2 minutes to toast the rice.

Reduce the heat to medium-low, pour in the beer and stir. Stir frequently until the beer has been completely absorbed, 3 to 4 minutes.

Add the salt, thyme, smoked paprika and cayenne pepper. Stir to combine.

Add the broth, ½ to 1 cup (120 to 240 ml) at a time. Stir frequently until the broth has been completely absorbed, about 5 minutes. Continue this process of adding a little bit of broth at a time, stirring and letting it absorb until all of the broth has been incorporated and the rice is cooked through and creamy.

Add the black-eyed peas. Stir to combine and cook for 3 to 4 minutes to heat the peas.

Taste and adjust the seasonings, adding the black pepper and more salt if needed.

Serve the risotto immediately with the rosemary on top.

Collard Green *Carbonara*

I am obsessed with making the perfect vegan carbonara. This southern version may have brought that obsession to an end. The sauce does an amazing job of mimicking the egg and cheese sauce that is traditional in a carbonara. The shiitake "bacon" provides the salty and sweet component while the collard greens take the dish to the next level. Time for me to retire as the self-appointed vegan carbonara tester—this is the recipe.

Serves: 6

8 oz (240 g) firm tofu

½ cup (120 ml) vegetable broth

2 tbsp (30 ml) dill pickle juice

¼ cup (15 g) nutritional yeast

½ tsp smoked paprika

½ tsp salt, plus more as necessary

Pinch of red pepper flakes

1 lb (450 g) linguine, fettuccine or spaghetti

2 tbsp (30 ml) olive oil

4 oz (120 g) shiitake mushrooms, thinly sliced

2 tbsp (30 ml) liquid aminos or soy sauce

1 tbsp (15 ml) liquid smoke

1 tbsp (15 ml) pure maple syrup

3 cups (108 g) finely chopped collard greens

Black pepper, to taste

Vegan Parmesan, as needed (optional)

Squeeze the tofu with your hands, removing as much moisture as you can. Add the tofu to a blender. Add the broth, pickle juice, nutritional yeast, smoked paprika, salt and red pepper flakes. Blend on high for 2 to 3 minutes, until the sauce is completely smooth. Set the sauce aside.

Cook the pasta according to package directions.

Heat the oil in a large nonstick skillet over medium-high heat. Add the mushrooms and sauté, reducing the heat as needed to prevent burning, for about 10 minutes, or until the mushrooms are starting to brown.

Add the liquid aminos, liquid smoke and maple syrup. Toss to coat the mushrooms.

Add the collard greens and toss to combine them with the mushrooms and seasonings. Sauté for about 10 minutes, or until the collard greens are tender. Season them with the salt and black pepper.

When the pasta is done, drain it and reserve the pasta water. Add the pasta to the skillet. Toss to combine the pasta with the mushrooms and collard greens.

Pour the sauce and ¼ cup (60 ml) of the reserved pasta water over the pasta. Toss to coat all of the pasta in the sauce. Add a little more pasta water if needed. Taste and adjust the seasonings.

Serve the carbonara topped with the Parmesan (if using).

Barbecue Mushroom *Lasagna*

This lasagna is the lasagna of my dreams, and let me assure you, I do a lot of dreaming about lasagna. Bursting with a barbecue mushroom filling, vegan béchamel sauce and no-boil lasagna noodles, this dish is bubbly, cheesy, decadent and oh, so classy.

Serves: 12

Barbecue Mushroom Filling

2 tbsp (30 ml) olive oil

2½ lbs (1.1 kg) cremini mushrooms, diced

6 cloves garlic, coarsely chopped

½ medium sweet onion, diced

Salt, to taste

Black pepper, to taste

1 cup (240 ml) Mustard Barbecue Sauce (page 58) or store-bought vegan barbecue sauce

1 cup (240 ml) vegetable broth

Béchamel Sauce

¼ cup (60 g) vegan butter

¼ cup (30 g) all-purpose flour

3 cups (720 ml) nondairy milk

¼ cup (15 g) nutritional yeast

1 tsp Dijon mustard

1 tsp fresh lemon juice

Salt, to taste

Black pepper, to taste

Lasagna

16 no-boil lasagna noodles

To make the barbecue mushroom filling, heat the oil in a large nonstick skillet over medium-high heat. Add the mushrooms, garlic and onion. Season the vegetables with salt and black pepper. Sauté for about 15 minutes, or until the mushrooms have released all their liquid and they are starting to brown. Reduce the heat as needed to prevent burning.

Add the barbecue sauce and broth. Stir to combine. Reduce the heat to low and simmer for 20 to 25 minutes, or until the sauce is very thick and the mushrooms are soft and brown. Taste and adjust the seasonings. Set the filling aside.

To make the béchamel sauce, melt the butter in a large nonstick skillet over medium-high heat. Whisk the flour into the butter to form a roux. Whisk the milk into the roux until there are no lumps left. Add the nutritional yeast, mustard, lemon juice, salt and black pepper.

Bring the sauce to a simmer, reduce the heat to low and cook, whisking frequently, until the sauce is thick, 2 to 3 minutes. Taste and adjust the seasonings.

In the bottom of a 13 x 9–inch (33 x 23–cm) baking dish, evenly spread out one-fourth of the mushroom filling. Spoon one-fourth of the béchamel sauce on top of the mushrooms, spreading the sauce out as evenly as possible. Place lasagna noodles on top of the béchamel, completely covering the sauce.

Repeat this process of layering mushrooms, béchamel sauce and noodles to create three layers of noodles. End with a layer of mushrooms and béchamel on top.

Preheat the oven to 375°F (191°C). Let the lasagna sit for 15 to 20 minutes while the oven preheats so the noodles can start absorbing the sauce.

Bake the lasagna for 30 to 40 minutes, or until the noodles are cooked through and the lasagna is bubbly on top. (Check the instructions on the package of lasagna noodles. Cooking times may vary.)

Let the lasagna cool for about 5 minutes before serving.

BAKED WHITE *Mac and Cheese*

This vegan mac and cheese is my favorite version of the dish. The cheese sauce is the creamiest, cheesiest, simplest sauce I have ever encountered on my vegan journey. This special mac and cheese is also topped with salty, crunchy pecans and breadcrumbs. There is nothing better.

Serves: 8

1 lb (450 g) elbow or shell macaroni

1 cup (110 g) raw cashews, soaked (see page 87)

1 cup (240 ml) nondairy milk

1 (15-oz [450-g]) block firm tofu

¼ cup (15 g) nutritional yeast

1 tsp Dijon mustard

1 tsp tahini

1 tsp fresh lemon juice

½ tsp garlic powder

¼ tsp ground nutmeg

1 tsp salt

½ tsp black pepper

1 cup (120 g) finely chopped roasted pecans

1 cup (55 g) panko breadcrumbs

2 tbsp (30 ml) olive oil

Preheat the oven to 375°F (191°C).

Cook the macaroni according to package directions.

While the macaroni is cooking, drain the soaked cashews and add them and the milk to a blender.

Squeeze the tofu with your hands, removing as much moisture as possible. Add the tofu to the blender.

Add the nutritional yeast, mustard, tahini, lemon juice, garlic powder, nutmeg, salt and black pepper to the blender. Blend on high for 2 to 3 minutes, scraping down the sides of the blender as needed, until the sauce is totally smooth. (If you are having a hard time blending the sauce, add a few splashes of milk until it is blending easily.) Set the sauce aside.

When the macaroni is done, drain it and return it to the pot.

Pour all of the cheese sauce into the pot with the macaroni and stir to combine. Taste and adjust the seasonings.

Pour the macaroni and cheese into a 13 x 9–inch (30 x 23–cm) baking dish. Smooth out the macaroni evenly.

In a small bowl, combine the pecans, breadcrumbs and oil. Toss to coat the pecans and breadcrumbs in the oil.

Top the macaroni and cheese with the pecans and breadcrumbs.

Bake for 10 to 15 minutes, or until the topping is crispy and brown.

Rather Fine FIXINS

When I go to a restaurant, I usually order a bunch of appetizers and side dishes. There is nothing better than a plethora of small plates to share. I love to do this not because I can't find anything else to eat, but because this way I can try as many things as humanly possible. The recipes in this chapter are appetizers and side dishes that anyone would want to eat as their main meal. They are that epic!

No southern meal is complete without the classic sides, but I think we can do a little better than those. In this chapter, you will find quintessential southern sides that have been elegantly updated. Hushpuppies, cornbread, grits, pasta salad, potato salad—everything you need for the most lavish dinner ever is right here. You just can't have a southern feast without these rather fine fixins!

CANDIED JALAPEÑO *Hushpuppies* WITH SWEET BUTTER

I grew up eating hushpuppies, and I will never turn one down. I've had some amazing hushpuppies in my time; however, these are the best of the best. They are moist on the inside, super crispy on the outside, and they're sweet with just a little spice. These are without a doubt the hushpuppies you will want to eat forever.

Serves: 6 to 8

4 medium jalapeños

¼ cup (48 g) vegan granulated sugar

2 tbsp (30 ml) water

1 cup (170 g) cornmeal

½ cup (60 g) all-purpose flour

2 tsp (8 g) baking powder

1 tsp salt

2 tbsp (18 g) cornstarch

¾ cup (180 ml) nondairy milk

⅓ cup (33 g) finely chopped scallions

Vegetable oil, as needed

SWEET BUTTER

⅓ cup (80 g) room-temperature vegan butter

1 tbsp (15 ml) agave syrup

Trim the stems from the jalapeños. Slice them down the center from top to bottom and scrape out the seeds with a spoon. Dice the jalapeños and add them to a small saucepan.

Add the sugar and water to the saucepan and cook over medium heat, stirring until the sugar has dissolved.

Reduce the heat to low and simmer the jalapeños until the liquid has thickened and candied the jalapeños, about 10 minutes. Turn off the heat (the liquid will thicken more as it cools). Let the candied jalapeños cool completely.

In a large bowl, stir together the cornmeal, flour, baking powder, salt and cornstarch. Pour in the milk and stir to fully combine.

If there is excess liquid in the saucepan containing the jalapeños, drain it. Fold the cooled candied jalapeños and scallions into the batter, making sure they are evenly distributed.

In a large skillet, heat 1½ to 2 inches (3.75 to 5 cm) of oil to 350°F (177°C). There should be tiny bubbles in the oil.

Drop large dollops of the batter into the hot oil, being sure not to overcrowd the skillet. Fry the hushpuppies on each side for about 2 minutes, or until they are golden brown. Place the hushpuppies on a paper towel when they are done, and repeat this process with the remaining batter.

Just before serving the hushpuppies, whisk together the butter and agave syrup in a small bowl.

Serve the hushpuppies with the sweet butter.

CREAMY GARLIC-TRUFFLE *Grits*

These are the classiest, most decadent grits ever. They feature a ton of garlic, they're incredibly velvety and they just happen to be dairy-free. Plus, they're finished with truffle oil because we are fancy people! Serve these grits alongside your favorite entrée, like Spicy Oven-Fried Tofu (page 36). They are also delicious topped with roasted vegetables or Barbecue Tempeh and Sweet Corn Pudding (page 65). Honestly, these grits are so mind-blowing, you may want to just sit down, right there in the kitchen, and eat an entire bowl.

Serves: 4

2 tsp (10 ml) olive oil

10 cloves garlic, finely chopped

4½ cups (1.1 L) almond milk or other nondairy milk

Salt, to taste

Black pepper, to taste

1 cup (170 g) grits

2 tbsp (30 g) vegan butter

1 tsp vegan truffle oil (see Note)

Finely chopped fresh chives, as needed

Heat the olive oil in a 2½-quart (2.4-L) saucepan over medium-high heat. Add the garlic and sauté, reducing the heat as needed to prevent burning, until the garlic is soft and beginning to brown, 3 to 4 minutes.

Add the milk and stir to combine with the garlic. Season the mixture with the salt and black pepper.

Bring the milk to a simmer, then reduce the heat to low. Very slowly, sprinkle the grits into the milk, whisking the entire time so the grits don't get lumpy (see Hot Tip). Season with more salt and black pepper.

Simmer the grits for 15 to 20 minutes, or until the grits are thick, creamy and completely cooked.

Turn off the heat and add the butter and truffle oil, whisking them into the hot grits. Taste and adjust the seasonings.

Top the grits with the chives and serve immediately.

Hot Tip: If your grits get lumpy, once they are cooked, use a hand mixer to smooth them out!

Note: While truffles are part of the fungi family (and thus vegan), they are often harvested with the help of pigs and dogs, who locate the truffles through scent. There is a large debate as to whether the animals are treated well while being kept to forage the truffles, so some people prefer to avoid consuming truffles. The good news for this recipe is that most truffle oil is vegan-friendly. Almost all of the truffle oil used today doesn't contain actual truffles. You can always be sure, though, by finding a truffle oil that specifies truffle flavor in the ingredients list instead of actual truffles.

SWEET 'N' SPICY *Cornbread*

If you were to ask me what I need on the side of every big plate of southern comfort food, I would say cornbread—hands down, every time. I don't want just any cornbread, though. I need moist, fluffy, flavorful cornbread. This sweet 'n' spicy version is anything but dry and bland. It is melt-in-your-mouth addictive—you'll want it on the side of every meal for the rest of your life.

Serves: 12

1 cup (120 g) all-purpose flour

1 tbsp (12 g) baking powder

1 tsp baking soda

1 tsp chili powder

½ tsp cayenne pepper

½ tsp smoked paprika

1 cup (170 g) cornmeal

½ cup (96 g) vegan sugar

1 tsp salt

2 tbsp (14 g) flax meal

3 tbsp (45 ml) water

1 cup (240 ml) nondairy milk

⅓ cup (80 ml) vegetable oil

¼ cup (60 ml) pure maple syrup

1 cup (144 g) fresh or canned corn (drained if canned)

Preheat the oven to 400°F (204°C).

In a large bowl, sift together the flour, baking powder, baking soda, chili powder, cayenne pepper and smoked paprika. Stir in the cornmeal, sugar and salt. Set the bowl aside.

In a small bowl, whisk together the flax meal and water. Set the mixture aside to thicken for 3 to 5 minutes.

In a medium bowl, whisk together the milk, oil and maple syrup.

Add the thickened flax meal to the milk mixture and whisk to combine. Add the milk-flax mixture to the flour mixture and stir to completely combine.

Add the corn to the batter, stirring gently so it is distributed evenly throughout the batter.

Spray a 9 x 13–inch (23 x 33–cm) baking dish with nonstick cooking spray, then pour the batter in.

Bake the cornbread for 20 to 25 minutes, or until a toothpick inserted into the center comes out clean.

Let the cornbread cool completely, then cut it into 12 squares and serve.

CHILI SMASHED *Potato Salad*

This potato salad is the pinnacle of greatness! The technique of boiling baby potatoes, smashing them and then baking them until they are crispy is my favorite thing to do. The outsides of these babies get so golden brown and crunchy. Toss them in a creamy chili sauce, and prepare yourself for the fact that you will never want a potato any other way again.

Serves: 6

2 tbsp (30 ml) olive oil, divided

3 lbs (1.4 kg) baby potatoes

Salt, to taste

Black pepper, to taste

¾ cup (165 g) vegan mayo

1 tbsp (15 ml) fresh lime juice

1 tsp chili powder

½ tsp smoked paprika

1 tsp agave syrup

⅓ cup (33 g) coarsely chopped scallions

Preheat the oven to 400°F (204°C). Grease a medium baking sheet with 1 tablespoon (15 ml) of the oil.

Place the potatoes in a large pot of cold water. Bring the water to a boil over high heat. Boil the potatoes until they are tender, 15 to 20 minutes. You should be able to smash a potato with a fork. Drain the potatoes and transfer them to the prepared baking sheet.

Using a cup (or anything that has a flat bottom), press down gently on a potato to smash it. Do not smash it completely flat—it should just pop open and be ¼ to ½ inch (6 to 13 mm) thick. Repeat this process with the remaining potatoes.

When all the potatoes are smashed, drizzle them with the remaining 1 tablespoon (15 ml) of oil and season them with salt and black pepper.

Bake the potatoes for 15 minutes, flip them and bake for 15 to 25 minutes more, or until they are very brown and crispy.

While the potatoes are baking, whisk together the mayo, lime juice, chili powder, smoked paprika, agave syrup, a pinch of salt and a pinch of black pepper in a large bowl. Set the sauce aside.

When the potatoes are done, remove them from the oven and let them cool, either slightly to serve as a warm potato salad or completely to serve as a chilled potato salad.

When the potatoes are cooled, add them to the sauce. Toss to coat the potatoes in the sauce.

Add the scallions, toss the potato salad and serve.

PIMENTO *Cheese Spread*

There is a chance that maybe, just maybe, this cashew-based spread is my favorite cheese. It is so creamy and so dippable. Spread this southern essential on crackers or veggies, put it on toast or bagels—however you want to serve it, every person who tries this cheese spread will never be the same. Who knew vegan cheese could be this jaw-droppingly amazing?

Serves: 4

1 cup (110 g) raw cashews, soaked (see page 87)

1 tbsp (15 g) tahini

3 tbsp (45 ml) fresh lemon juice

¼ cup (60 g) solid coconut oil

¼ cup (60 ml) water

1 tsp salt, plus more as needed

1 tsp onion powder

1 tsp garlic powder

¼ cup (44 g) diced pimentos

1 tbsp (15 g) sweet relish

3 scallions, finely chopped

Pinch of cayenne pepper

Crackers or vegetables, as needed

Drain the soaked cashews and add them to a blender. Add the tahini, lemon juice, coconut oil, water and salt.

Blend on high for 3 to 5 minutes, scraping down the sides of the blender as needed, until the cheese mixture is completely smooth.

When the cheese mixture is totally smooth, transfer it to a medium bowl. Add the onion powder, garlic powder, pimentos, sweet relish, scallions, cayenne pepper and salt to taste. Stir to combine. Taste and adjust the seasonings.

Chill the pimento cheese spread in the fridge for at least 1 hour—the cheese will firm up once it's chilled.

If you want a thick and firm cheese, serve it right out of the fridge; if you want a softer cheese, bring it to room temperature before serving. Serve with crackers or vegetables.

Hot Tip: This cashew cheese base is great for all kinds of different flavors. You can use it with any add-ins you want, like garlic and herbs.

THE YUMMIEST FRIED *Pickles*

I like to consider myself a fried pickle connoisseur. I have had all kinds of fried pickles in many different locations, and I have three qualifications for a good fried pickle. First, pickle chips are preferable to spears. With pickle spears, I feel like the crunchy-fried-goodness-to-pickle ratio is off. Second, the simpler the better. Just a salty, slightly spicy, crispy outside is best. Third, fried pickles must be served with awesome dips. These check off all those boxes and yes, they are the yummiest.

Serves: 6

3 cups (459 g) dill pickle chips

Vegetable oil, as needed

1 cup (240 ml) soy milk or other nondairy milk

1 tsp fresh lemon juice

2 cups (240 g) all-purpose flour

2 tsp salt

¼ tsp cayenne pepper

¼ tsp smoked paprika

White Barbecue Sauce (page 46)

Mississippi Comeback Sauce (page 78)

Place the pickles on some paper towels and top them with more paper towels. Press down gently to dry them a bit.

In a medium pot over medium-high heat, bring about ½ inch (13 mm) of the oil to 350°F (177°C). Reduce the heat if needed to maintain the temperature of the oil.

In a medium bowl, stir together the milk and lemon juice. Set the mixture aside to thicken.

In another medium bowl, whisk together the flour, salt, cayenne pepper and smoked paprika. Place this bowl next to the bowl containing the milk-lemon mixture.

Place 5 or 6 pickles into the flour mixture, coat the pickles completely and shake off the extra flour. Dip the pickles into the milk mixture, then dip them back into the flour. Shake off the extra flour. Repeat this process with the remaining pickles.

Fry the pickles in small batches for 1 to 2 minutes on each side, until they are golden brown. Transfer the fried pickles to dry paper towels to drain.

Serve the pickles immediately with the White Barbecue Sauce and Mississippi Comeback Sauce.

Au Gratin Hash Brown Casserole

This simple casserole is also known as funeral potatoes, a name that originated from a widespread tradition of bringing this piping-hot, comfort-food casserole to gatherings after funerals. My hash brown casserole is cheesy, creamy and good enough to bring to any event (not just funerals). It is a holiday staple in my house, and I promise it is soon to be a staple in yours as well!

Serves: 10

2 tbsp (30 g) vegan butter

1 cup (150 g) diced yellow onion

1 cup (110 g) raw cashews, soaked (see page 87)

1 cup (240 ml) vegetable broth

½ cup (120 ml) nondairy milk

¼ cup (15 g) nutritional yeast

1 tsp Dijon mustard

Salt, to taste

Black pepper, to taste

2 tbsp (16 g) all-purpose flour

2 lbs (900 g) frozen hash browns, thawed

2½ cups (63 g) cornflakes, crushed

2 tbsp (30 ml) olive oil

Finely chopped scallions or fresh chives, as needed

Preheat the oven to 400°F (204°C). Spray a 13 x 9–inch (33 x 23–cm) baking dish with nonstick cooking spray.

In a medium saucepan over medium heat, melt the butter. Add the onion and sauté, reducing the heat as needed to prevent burning, for 8 to 10 minutes, or until the onion is very soft and translucent.

While the onion is sautéing, drain the soaked cashews and add them to a blender. Add the broth, milk, nutritional yeast, mustard, salt and black pepper. Blend on high for 3 to 5 minutes, scraping down the sides of the blender if needed, until the sauce is completely smooth. Set the sauce aside.

Add the flour to the onion and stir to coat the onion in the flour and form a paste.

Add the sauce to the onion-flour mixture and whisk to combine. Remove the saucepan from the heat and whisk the sauce constantly for 1 to 2 minutes, until it is thick and smooth.

Place the hash browns in a large bowl and season them with salt and black pepper. Pour the sauce on top of the hash browns. Toss to fully combine.

Scoop the mixture into the prepared baking dish. Smooth out the hash browns evenly.

Bake the casserole for 30 minutes. Remove the casserole from the oven.

In a small bowl, combine the cornflakes and oil.

Top the casserole evenly with the cornflake mixture, and bake for 10 to 15 minutes, or until the topping is brown and crispy.

Top the casserole with the scallions and serve.

DILL PICKLE *Pasta Salad*

My love affair with pasta salad developed slowly. I hated the kind my mom used to make when I was a kid. It tasted like nothing but celery and mayo. It wasn't until I realized I could do anything with pasta salad that I became enamored with the idea of creating the perfect plant-based version! This recipe is the amalgamation of everything I love about pasta salad.

Serves: 6

1 lb (450 g) pasta (any short variety)

1½ cups (330 g) vegan mayo

2 tbsp (30 ml) apple cider vinegar

1 tbsp (15 ml) agave syrup

2 tsp (10 g) Dijon mustard

Salt, to taste

Black pepper, to taste

½ cup (75 g) diced sweet onion

1 cup (153 g) coarsely chopped dill pickles

1 tbsp (3 g) finely chopped fresh dill

Cook the pasta according to package directions. When the pasta is done, drain it and let it cool to room temperature. (I like to run cold water over the pasta to speed up the cooling process.)

Meanwhile, in a large bowl, whisk together the mayo, vinegar, agave syrup, mustard, salt and black pepper. Whisk until the dressing is fully combined and smooth.

Add the cooled pasta to the dressing and stir to completely coat the pasta in the dressing. Add the onion, pickles and dill. Toss to combine. Season with salt and black pepper. Taste and adjust the seasonings.

Serve the pasta salad immediately or place it in the fridge to chill completely before serving.

QUICK SPICY PICKLED *Green Beans*

Pickles are my favorite thing and green beans are my second favorite thing. Basically, these pickled green beans are all I've ever wanted in life. They make the perfect finger food to serve at your southern-inspired picnic or cookout. They're spicy, sweet, crunchy and so good you won't be able to stop yourself from walking back to the table to get another and another. Good thing this recipe will feed a crowd!

Serves: 6 to 8

1 lb (450 g) fresh green beans, cleaned and trimmed

1 cup (240 ml) distilled white vinegar

1 cup (240 ml) apple cider vinegar

1 tbsp (12 g) vegan sugar

1 tsp salt

2 cloves garlic, smashed

½ tsp red pepper flakes

1 tbsp (3 g) coarsely chopped fresh dill

1 tbsp (3 g) coarsely chopped fresh chives

Snap any large green beans in half. Leave any smaller ones whole. Place the green beans in a heatproof container.

In a small saucepan over medium heat, combine the distilled white vinegar, apple cider vinegar, sugar, salt, garlic, red pepper flakes, dill and chives. Bring the mixture to a simmer and stir just until the sugar and salt dissolve, 1 to 2 minutes.

Remove the saucepan from the heat and immediately pour the pickling liquid over the green beans.

Stir the green beans and make sure they are submerged in the liquid. (If the container is shallow and doesn't allow them to be submerged, stir them every few hours.)

Let the green beans cool to room temperature. Transfer them to the fridge to chill for at least 8 hours before serving.

The green beans will keep for about 2 weeks, covered, in the fridge.

Hot Tip: You can use this method to make any pickled veggies you want!

Sweet Home SOUPS

During my formative years, I was convinced soup was boring and awful. I thought all soups were condensed and from a can. It wasn't until culinary school that I realized I'd been doing soup wrong for so long.

The soups, stews, chowders and bisques in this chapter honor all things southern and will give you that "Oh, dang" moment. From classic sweet potatoes and corn to down-home dumplings and smoke, you'll find all kinds of warm and soothing rainy-day dishes here. The heartiness in these recipes will convince you soup is the best comfort meal. The creamy goodness will make dairy a distant memory. The flavors will make you dance around your kitchen while stirring the pot and sneaking a little more than just a taste. And the ease of making these recipes will have you serving them up again and again.

SAGE AND VEGGIE DUMPLING *Stew*

Getting a spoonful of this inviting stew and a bit of the tender sage dumplings all in one bite is like knowing what true love is. Sage is my essential cool-weather herb—its peppery taste and delicious fragrance remind me of the perfect southern fall. This dish is easily customized to add your favorite veggies, and guess what? No mushy dumplings here!

Serves: 4 to 6

VEGETABLE STEW

1 tbsp (15 ml) olive oil

6 cloves garlic, finely chopped

½ medium Vidalia onion, finely chopped

Salt, to taste

Black pepper, to taste

2 large russet potatoes, diced

10 oz (300 g) cremini mushrooms, thickly sliced

3 large carrots, coarsely chopped

5 cups (1.2 L) vegetable broth

2 tbsp (30 ml) soy sauce or liquid aminos

2 tsp (10 ml) agave syrup (optional)

1 tsp dried sage

¼ tsp dried thyme

SAGE DUMPLINGS

1⅓ cups (160 g) all-purpose flour

2 tsp (8 g) baking powder

1 tsp baking soda

1 tsp salt

1 tsp dried sage

⅔ cup (160 ml) nondairy milk

1 tbsp (15 ml) olive oil

To make the vegetable stew, heat the oil in a large pot over medium heat. Add the garlic and onion. Sauté for about 5 minutes, reducing the heat as needed to prevent burning, or until the onion is starting to caramelize. Season the garlic and onion with the salt and black pepper.

Add the potatoes, mushrooms and carrots. Stir to combine, and season the vegetables with salt and black pepper. Sauté for 1 to 2 minutes.

Add the broth, soy sauce and agave syrup (if using). Stir to combine. Add the sage and thyme.

Increase the heat to medium-high and bring the stew to a simmer. Reduce the heat to medium-low, cover the pot and simmer for 30 minutes, or until the vegetables are soft.

While the stew is simmering, prepare the sage dumplings. In a large bowl, sift together the flour, baking powder and baking soda. Add the salt and sage.

Stir the milk and oil into the flour mixture until fully combined. Set the dumpling batter aside.

When the vegetables are cooked through, season the stew with a bit more salt and black pepper. Taste and adjust the seasonings.

Reduce the heat to low and drop 1- to 2-tablespoon (15- to 30-g) lumps of the dumpling batter all over the top of the stew.

Cover the pot and simmer for 10 to 15 minutes, or until a toothpick inserted into the center of a dumpling comes out clean. Serve immediately.

Smoky Sweet Potato *Soup*

This delicious, thick and creamy sweet potato soup tastes like it was cooked all day with bacon. But in reality, it's made in a flash and that smoky flavor is from all the rockin' seasonings you add. This is what cozy and comforting looks, feels and tastes like.

Serves: 4

1 tbsp (15 ml) olive oil

4 cloves garlic, finely chopped

½ medium sweet onion, diced

2 lbs (900 g) sweet potatoes, diced

2 tbsp (30 ml) pure maple syrup

2 tbsp (30 ml) soy sauce or liquid aminos

1 tbsp (15 ml) liquid smoke

1 tsp smoked paprika

Salt, to taste

8 cups (1.9 L) vegetable broth, divided

Black pepper, to taste

Scallions, for topping (optional)

Heat the oil in a large pot over medium-high heat. Add the garlic, onion and sweet potatoes. Sauté for about 10 minutes, or until the sweet potatoes are getting brown and starting to soften.

Add the maple syrup, soy sauce, liquid smoke, smoked paprika and a pinch of salt to the pot. Stir to coat the vegetables with the seasonings, then sauté for 5 minutes.

Add 6 cups (1.4 L) of the broth and a few pinches of salt and black pepper.

Bring the mixture to a simmer, then reduce the heat to medium-low. Simmer for 10 to 15 minutes, or until the sweet potatoes can easily be smashed with a fork.

Turn off the heat and transfer the soup to a blender. Blend on high until the soup is completely smooth (see Hot Tip), then transfer the soup back to the pot. You may also use an immersion blender to blend the soup in the pot.

Turn the heat to low. Add the remaining 2 cups (480 ml) of broth and stir to combine. Season the soup with more salt and black pepper. Simmer for 5 minutes. Taste and adjust the seasonings, then serve. Top with scallions, if desired.

Hot Tip: If you use a blender to blend the hot soup, make sure you remove the small cap that is in the center of blender's lid and cover the hole with a kitchen towel or paper towel. Often, if you blend something hot without leaving the blender jar open a bit, whatever is in the blender will explode out of the top of the jar.

PANHANDLE *Chowder*

My family and I currently live in the Florida Panhandle, and we take frequent trips to Panama City Beach and Pensacola. All along the coast, you can find restaurants with a seafood chowder aptly named Panhandle chowder. This recipe is my tribute to some of my favorite places. The mushrooms and kelp powder are used to mimic seafood, and the liquid smoke mimics the bacon flavor. The cashews and nondairy milk provide the creamy texture every chowder needs—this is so thick and yummy, you may shed a tear.

Serves: 4

2 tbsp (30 ml) olive oil

2 cups (450 g) diced russet potatoes

10 oz (300 g) cremini mushrooms, diced

2 medium ribs celery, finely chopped

1 small white onion, diced

4 cloves garlic, finely chopped

1 tsp dried thyme

1 tsp liquid smoke

Salt, to taste

Black pepper, to taste

1 cup (110 g) raw cashews, soaked (see page 87)

1½ cups (360 ml) nondairy milk

1 tbsp (9 g) cornstarch

¼ cup (60 ml) vegan white wine

4 cups (960 ml) vegetable broth

1–2 tsp (2–4 g) kelp powder

Lemon wedges (optional)

Crackers or bread, as needed

Heat the oil in a large pot over medium-high heat. Add the potatoes, mushrooms, celery, onion, garlic, thyme and liquid smoke. Season the mixture with a pinch of the salt and a pinch of the black pepper. Sauté the vegetables for about 10 minutes, reducing the heat as needed to prevent burning.

Meanwhile, drain the soaked cashews and add them to a blender. Add the milk and cornstarch to the blender. Blend on high for 3 to 5 minutes, scraping down the sides of the blender as needed, until the cashew cream is completely smooth. Season the cashew cream with a pinch of salt and a pinch of black pepper. Set the cashew cream aside.

When the onion is translucent and the potatoes are starting to soften, add the wine to the pot and stir, scraping up any bits that are stuck to the bottom of the pot. Add the broth, bring the chowder to a simmer and reduce the heat to low. Simmer for 15 to 20 minutes, or until the potatoes are cooked through.

Pour the cashew cream into the pot and whisk to combine. Sprinkle in the kelp powder, using 1 teaspoon if you want a mild seafood flavor or 2 teaspoons (4 g) if you want a stronger seafood flavor. Simmer for 3 to 5 minutes, or until the chowder is thick.

Season the chowder with additional salt and black pepper. Taste and adjust the seasonings.

Serve the chowder with a squeeze of lemon (if using) and crackers.

Hot Tip: If you don't cook with alcohol, I have made this recipe without the wine as well, and it still turns out perfect—feel free to leave the wine out.

Lobster Mushroom and Corn *Bisque*

Creamy, sweet and a little spicy, this bisque is intensely delicious. I loved lobster bisque when I was a kid, and this easy-to-make version is so much better. The lobster mushrooms are luscious and make this recipe taste like the real deal. You may want to eat this bisque for every meal, or name your firstborn child after it.

Serves: 4

1 cup (110 g) raw cashews, soaked (see page 87)

5 cups (1.2 L) vegetable broth, divided

1 tbsp (15 ml) fresh lemon juice

Salt, to taste

Black pepper, to taste

1 tbsp (15 ml) olive oil

1 large carrot, coarsely chopped

½ medium sweet onion, finely chopped

3 cloves garlic, finely chopped

1 cup (175 g) fresh, thawed frozen or drained canned corn kernels

1 cup (36 g) dried lobster mushrooms, soaked in warm water for 1 to 2 hours

2 tbsp (30 g) tomato paste

1 cup (240 ml) vegan white wine

2 sprigs fresh thyme

Pinch of cayenne pepper

Drain the soaked cashews and add them to a blender. Add 1 cup (240 ml) of the broth, lemon juice and a pinch of salt and a pinch of black pepper. Blend on high for 3 to 5 minutes, scraping down the sides of the blender as needed, until the cashew cream is completely smooth. Set the cashew cream aside.

In a large pot, heat the oil over medium-high heat. Add the carrot, onion and garlic. Sprinkle the vegetables with a pinch of salt and a pinch of black pepper. Sauté, reducing the heat as needed to prevent burning, until the onion becomes translucent, 3 to 5 minutes.

Add the corn and mushrooms. Sauté for about 5 minutes to cook the corn and mushrooms. Add another pinch of salt and black pepper. Add the tomato paste and stir it into the vegetables.

Pour the wine into the pot and stir, scraping any browned bits from the bottom of the pot.

Add the thyme and pour the remaining 4 cups (960 ml) of broth into the pot.

Add the cashew cream and season the bisque with salt and black pepper. Stir to combine.

Bring the bisque to a simmer. Reduce the heat to low and simmer for 10 to 15 minutes to develop the flavors and cook off the wine.

Transfer the bisque to a blender and blend the bisque until it's completely smooth. (You may also use an immersion blender to blend the bisque in the pot.) Return the bisque to the pot. Add the cayenne pepper. Taste and adjust the seasonings.

Serve the bisque immediately.

Mac 'n' Cheese *Soup*

There is not a single person in this world who doesn't need this creamy soup in their life. Let me make my case. First, you only need ten easy-to-find, totally normal ingredients. Second, it is probably the easiest soup ever. Third, after you taste this soup, you will never be the same. The world will look different—a little brighter, a little more delicious and so much happier. Just trust me, this soup is where it's at.

Serves: 4

Cashew Cheese Sauce

1 cup (110 g) raw cashews, soaked (see page 87)

1 cup (240 ml) vegetable broth

¼ cup (15 g) nutritional yeast

1 tbsp (15 ml) fresh lemon juice

Pinch of salt

Pinch of black pepper

Soup

4 tsp (20 ml) olive oil, divided

6 large cloves garlic, finely chopped

6 cups (1.4 L) vegetable broth

1 tsp Dijon mustard

Salt, to taste

Black pepper, to taste

1–1½ cups (115–173 g) elbow or shell macaroni

1 cup (55 g) panko breadcrumbs

1 tsp Italian seasoning

To make the cashew cheese sauce, drain the soaked cashews and add them to a blender. Add the broth, nutritional yeast, lemon juice, salt and black pepper. Blend for 3 to 5 minutes, scraping down the sides of the blender as needed, until the sauce is completely smooth. Set the sauce aside.

To make the soup, heat 2 teaspoons (10 ml) of oil in a large pot over medium-high heat. Add the garlic and sauté for 1 to 2 minutes, until the garlic is soft.

Add the broth, mustard and cashew cheese sauce. Stir to combine. Season the mixture with the salt and black pepper and bring it to a boil. Reduce the heat to medium-low and simmer.

Add the macaroni, using 1 cup (115 g) if you want the soup to be thinner and 1½ cups (173 g) if you want the soup to be thicker.

Simmer the soup for 6 to 9 minutes, stirring frequently, or until the macaroni is cooked.

While the soup is simmering, heat the remaining 2 teaspoons (10 ml) of oil in a small nonstick skillet over medium-low heat.

Add the panko breadcrumbs and Italian seasoning. Stir to combine and coat the breadcrumbs with the oil. Cook for 2 to 4 minutes, stirring frequently, until they are brown.

When the macaroni is cooked through, taste the soup and adjust the seasonings. Top the soup with the toasted breadcrumbs and serve immediately.

Hot Tip: The macaroni will get mushy if the soup sits around for a long time. If you want to make this soup ahead of time, make the broth and add the macaroni right before serving.

Deep
SOUTH *Desserts*

You may or may not know this, but I'm a trained pastry chef. So, I don't mean to toot my own horn or anything, but dessert is kind of my specialty. Here you will find all of my favorite southern desserts with a unique, "Lauren" spin on them. This chapter boasts puddings, pies, cobblers, cheesecake and of course some fried goodies, all vegan! I am madly in love with each of these desserts. They're the culmination of everything I love about baking and pastries, and there is something for everyone, from the seasoned baker to someone who has never used an oven before. Needless to say, I'm pretty pumped about all the incredible desserts in this chapter!

BANANA SPLIT SUGAR-DUSTED *Beignets*

These beignets are a tribute to one of my favorite places in the world: New Orleans. We are only a five- or six-hour drive away, and my whole family loves the city. These beignets taste just like the ones from Café Du Monde. I had to make them even more awesome by drowning them in chocolate powdered sugar, banana powdered sugar and strawberry powdered sugar. They taste just like a banana split!

Serves: 6

1¼ cups (300 ml) warm water (about 110°F [43°C]; see Hot Tip on page 134)

2¼ tsp (7 g) active dry yeast

¼ cup (48 g) vegan granulated sugar

2 tbsp (30 ml) vegetable oil, plus more as needed

3½ cups (420 g) all-purpose flour, plus more as needed

1 tbsp (9 g) cornstarch

1 tsp salt

1 cup (130 g) powdered vegan sugar, divided

1 cup (140 g) freeze-dried strawberries

1 cup (140 g) freeze-dried bananas

2 tbsp (14 g) cocoa powder

Pour the warm water into a large bowl or the bowl of a stand mixer. Sprinkle the yeast into the warm water. Then sprinkle the granulated sugar on top of the yeast.

Let the yeast bloom for 5 minutes. The yeast should start to bubble and form big bubbles of yeast at the top of the water.

Add the oil to the yeast and water mixture.

In a large bowl, sift together the flour, cornstarch and salt.

Add the flour mixture to the water mixture a little at a time, using a dough hook (if you are using a stand mixer) or stirring with a spoon to combine.

When all the flour mixture has been added, knead the dough either with the dough hook in the stand mixer or your hands on a floured surface for 1 to 2 minutes, until the dough has formed a soft, smooth ball.

Leave the dough in the bowl and cover it with a kitchen towel. Let the dough rise in a warm place for 1 hour.

While the dough is rising, add ¼ cup (33 g) of the powdered sugar and the strawberries to a food processor. Pulse until the strawberries turn into a powder and are combined with the powdered sugar. Transfer the strawberry powdered sugar to a medium bowl and wipe out the food processor. Set the strawberry powdered sugar aside.

Add ¼ cup (33 g) of the powdered sugar and the bananas to the food processor. Pulse until the bananas turn into a powder and are combined with the powdered sugar. Transfer the banana powdered sugar to another medium bowl. Set the banana powdered sugar aside.

Add the remaining ½ cup (65 g) of powdered sugar and cocoa powder to a medium bowl and whisk to combine. Set the chocolate powdered sugar aside.

(Continued)

Banana Split Sugar-Dusted Beignets
(Continued)

Once the dough has risen, transfer the dough to a floured work surface. Put some flour on top of the dough to make sure it isn't sticky. Roll the dough into a rectangle that is about ½ inch (13 mm) thick.

Cut the dough into 2 x 3–inch (5 x 7.5–cm) rectangles. Let them rise for about 5 minutes. While the beignets rise, heat the oil.

In a large skillet over high heat, bring about 1 inch (2.5 cm) of oil to 350°F (177°C). Reduce the heat as needed to maintain the oil's temperature.

Place 3 or 4 beignets at a time in the skillet. Fry them for about 2 minutes per side or until they are golden brown. Put the fried beignets on a paper towel to drain. Repeat this process with the remaining beignets.

Serve the beignets freshly fried and covered in your choice of the strawberry, banana or chocolate powdered sugar.

Hot Tip: You will be able to tell if the water is the right temperature by touch. If it is too hot to stick your finger in, it will kill the yeast. It should feel warm, but it should not burn your finger.

MISSISSIPPI MUD *Cheesecake*

This is the best vegan chocolate cheesecake. It has a unique graham cracker and chocolate cookie crust, and it's almost obnoxiously smothered with roasted, salted pecans, marshmallows and dark chocolate. This cheesecake is legit and the most amazing tribute to traditional Mississippi mud desserts. I can assure you that you won't know the difference between this masterpiece and a cheesecake made with dairy.

Serves: 8 to 10

CRUST

1 cup (90 g) vegan graham cracker crumbs

2 cups (180 g) vegan chocolate sandwich cookie crumbs

2 tbsp (18 g) vegan brown sugar

½ cup (120 g) vegan butter, melted

CHEESECAKE BATTER

1 lb (450 g) firm tofu

1 lb (450 g) vegan cream cheese

¼ cup (60 ml) nondairy milk, plus more as needed

½ cup (120 ml) pure maple syrup

2 tsp (10 ml) pure vanilla extract

1 cup (192 g) vegan granulated sugar

½ cup (56 g) cocoa powder

1 tbsp (9 g) cornstarch

⅓ cup (40 g) all-purpose flour

Pinch of salt

To make the crust, preheat the oven to 350°F (177°C). Spray an 8-inch (20-cm) springform pan with nonstick cooking spray.

In a large bowl, combine the graham cracker crumbs, cookie crumbs, brown sugar and butter. Stir to fully combine, making sure the butter is evenly distributed so the crust will hold together.

Pour the cookie crust into the prepared pan.

Press the crust firmly into the pan, distributing it evenly all the way around the pan. (I like to use the bottom of a cup to press it down.)

Bake the crust for 8 to 10 minutes. It will start to brown on the edges.

In the meantime, make the cheesecake batter. Using your hands, squeeze as much liquid out of the tofu as possible. Add the tofu, cream cheese, milk, maple syrup, vanilla, granulated sugar, cocoa powder, cornstarch, flour and salt to a blender.

Blend the mixture on high for 3 to 5 minutes, until the cheesecake filling is completely smooth, scraping the sides of the blender down as needed. (If the mixture is having a hard time blending, add a bit more milk.)

(Continued)

Mississippi Mud Cheesecake (Continued)

TOPPINGS

1 cup (120 g) coarsely chopped roasted salted pecans

1 cup (50 g) mini or coarsely chopped vegan marshmallows

8 oz (240 g) vegan dark chocolate

1 tsp solid coconut oil

Remove the crust from the oven and set it aside. Increase the oven temperature to 375°F (191°C).

Pour the batter into the crust and smooth it out. Bake the cheesecake for 45 minutes.

Remove the cheesecake from the oven. Top it with the pecans and marshmallows, spreading them evenly over the entire top of the cheesecake.

Bake the cheesecake for another 10 to 15 minutes, or until the marshmallows are brown and the cheesecake seems slightly jiggly in the center. (It will firm as it cools.)

Chill the cheesecake in the refrigerator for at least 4 hours. Once it has cooled, add the dark chocolate to a small saucepan over low heat. Stir the chocolate until it has melted. Turn off the heat and stir in the coconut oil.

Drizzle the chocolate all over the top of the cheesecake. Let the chocolate set up for 5 minutes.

Remove the side from the springform pan. Cut the cheesecake and serve.

CHOCOLATE PUDDING AND PEANUT BUTTER MOUSSE *Pie*

Is there a person among us who doesn't salivate at the sight and smell of anything that combines chocolate and peanut butter? This mouth party is brought to you in the form of creamy chocolate, light and fluffy peanut butter and a crunchy crust. Bring the balloons and get ready to party.

Serves: 8 to 10

CRUST

2½ cups (225 g) vegan graham cracker crumbs

3 tbsp (27 g) vegan brown sugar

1 cup (240 g) vegan butter, melted

CHOCOLATE PUDDING

2 cups (480 ml) nondairy milk

3 tbsp (27 g) cornstarch

½ cup (120 ml) pure maple syrup

½ cup (56 g) cocoa powder

1 tsp pure vanilla extract

Pinch of salt

PEANUT BUTTER MOUSSE

1 cup (180 g) creamy peanut butter

¾ cup (98 g) vegan powdered sugar

2 tsp (10 ml) pure vanilla extract

¼ tsp salt

8–9 oz (240–270 g) Coconut Whipped Cream (page 151) or store-bought vegan whipped topping, plus more as needed

Preheat the oven to 350°F (177°C).

To make the crust, in a large bowl, stir together the graham cracker crumbs and brown sugar. Add the butter to the crumb mixture and stir to combine, making sure the butter has soaked into all of the graham cracker crumbs.

Transfer the crumbs to a 9-inch (23-cm) pie pan. Press the crumbs evenly into the pie pan. (I like to use a cup to make sure the crumbs are tightly packed into the pie pan.)

Bake the crust for 12 to 15 minutes, or until it is brown and firm.

Let the crust cool while you make the chocolate pudding. In a medium bowl, whisk together the milk and cornstarch, making sure the cornstarch has completely dissolved in the milk to prevent a lumpy pudding.

Transfer the milk to a small saucepan over medium-low heat. Add the maple syrup, cocoa powder, vanilla and salt. Whisk to combine.

Bring the mixture to a simmer, whisking frequently. Reduce the heat to low and simmer for 1 to 3 minutes, or until the pudding is thick.

Pour the pudding into the cooled crust and smooth it out evenly. Chill the pie in the refrigerator for 1 hour.

To make the peanut butter mousse, combine the peanut butter, powdered sugar, vanilla and salt in a large bowl or the bowl of a stand mixer. Mix until the ingredients are combined. Fold in the Coconut Whipped Cream.

Pour the peanut butter mousse over the chocolate pudding and smooth it out. Chill the pie in the refrigerator for at least 2 hours.

When you are ready to serve the pie, top it with additional Coconut Whipped Cream.

Keep the pie refrigerated.

PECAN PRALINE *Bars*

These bars are the crispy, crunchy, sweet and salty dessert you've been fantasizing about. They are probably the easiest dessert of all time and taste just like a classic praline—except these are even better, since the praline mixture is poured over graham crackers. With the extreme crunch from the bottom layer of graham crackers and the salty caramel top, these bars are otherworldly.

Serves: 12

28–30 vegan graham cracker halves

½ cup (120 ml) pure maple syrup

¼ cup (36 g) vegan brown sugar

½ cup (120 g) vegan butter

1 tsp pure vanilla extract

½ tsp salt

1½ cups (180 g) roasted pecans, coarsely chopped

Preheat the oven to 350°F (177°C). Spray an 18 x 13–inch (45 x 33–cm) baking sheet with nonstick cooking spray.

Arrange the graham crackers in a single layer to cover the entire baking sheet.

In a small saucepan over medium heat, combine the maple syrup, brown sugar, butter, vanilla and salt. Stir to combine and heat until the ingredients are melted.

Bring the mixture to a simmer, reduce the heat to low and simmer for 2 to 4 minutes to thicken the mixture slightly and create the caramel topping.

Remove the saucepan from the heat and stir the pecans into the caramel.

Pour the caramel mixture over the graham crackers and smooth it out to evenly coat all of the graham crackers as much as possible.

Bake the bars for 8 to 10 minutes, or until the caramel is all bubbly and has coated all of the graham crackers.

Let the bars cool completely. When they are cooled and firm, break them into individual bars.

Keep the bars refrigerated until you are ready to serve.

RED VELVET *Funnel Cakes*

My house is a crazy carnival, and I'm really into embracing that atmosphere by frying up some of these crispy, sweet red velvet funnel cakes. They take no time at all, and soon you'll be living in a perfect world—one where there is a year-round fair in your home, and that fair inexplicably serves vegan red velvet funnel cakes. Yup, this can be your life.

Serves: 6

1½ cups (360 ml) nondairy milk

1 tsp distilled white vinegar

2 cups (240 g) all-purpose flour

2 tbsp (14 g) cocoa powder

1 tsp baking powder

½ tsp baking soda

2 tbsp (18 g) cornstarch

1 tsp salt

⅓ cup (64 g) vegan granulated sugar

1 tsp pure vanilla extract

1 tbsp (15 ml) natural vegan red food coloring

Vegetable oil, as needed

Vegan powdered sugar, as needed

Coconut Whipped Cream (page 151) or store-bought vegan whipped topping, as needed

In a small bowl, whisk together the milk and vinegar. Let the mixture sit for 2 to 3 minutes.

In a large bowl, sift together the flour, cocoa powder, baking powder, baking soda and cornstarch. Stir in the salt and granulated sugar. Set the bowl aside.

Whisk the vanilla and food coloring into the milk mixture. Pour the milk mixture into the flour mixture and whisk to fully combine.

In a large pot or skillet, bring 1 to 2 inches (2.5 to 5 cm) of the oil to 350 to 375°F (177 to 191°C). Reduce the heat as needed to maintain the oil's temperature.

Pour the batter into a large plastic bag. Cut off the tip of the corner of the bag's bottom. Make sure it is a very small opening, or the batter will pour out too fast.

Hold the bag of batter over the hot oil and begin to drizzle the batter into the oil, swirling fresh batter back and forth across the frying batter. Make the funnel cake as big as you want.

Fry the funnel cake for 2 to 3 minutes on one side, then flip it and fry it for 2 to 3 minutes on the other side, until the funnel cake is crispy.

Place each funnel cake on a paper towel to drain and repeat the preceding process with the rest of the batter.

Serve the funnel cakes with lots of powdered sugar, vegan whipped topping or both.

Fluffy Triple-Berry *Shortcake*

I feel like I could eat these fluffy little shortcakes covered in sweet berries every day and never get tired of them. I put a bit of a spin on traditional strawberry shortcakes and made this shortcake lighter and airier. Then to make life even better, I used blackberries, blueberries and cherries! If you make these for guests, don't be alarmed if you see them closing their eyes and shoveling these shortcakes into their mouths. It's necessary.

Serves: 3 to 6

1 cup (144 g) fresh blackberries, sliced in half

1 cup (100 g) fresh blueberries

1 cup (225 g) fresh cherries, pitted and sliced in half

¼ cup (48 g) plus 3 tbsp (36 g) vegan sugar, divided

2 cups (240 g) all-purpose flour

2 tsp (8 g) baking powder

½ tsp baking soda

1 tsp salt

1 cup (240 ml) canned coconut cream or full-fat coconut milk

½ cup (120 ml) nondairy milk

Coconut Whipped Cream (page 151) or store-bought vegan whipped topping (optional)

Preheat the oven to 400°F (204°C). Spray an 8 x 8–inch (20 x 20–cm) baking pan with nonstick cooking spray.

Combine the blackberries, blueberries and cherries in a medium bowl. Sprinkle ¼ cup (48 g) of the sugar on top of the blackberry mixture and toss the berries to coat them all in the sugar. Transfer the bowl to the fridge.

Sift the flour, baking powder and baking soda into a large bowl. Add the remaining 3 tablespoons (36 g) of sugar and salt.

Add the coconut cream and milk to the flour mixture. Whisk until fully combined.

Pour the batter into the prepared baking pan. Spread it out evenly.

Bake the shortcake for 15 to 18 minutes, or until the shortcake is golden brown and a toothpick inserted into the center comes out clean.

Let the shortcake cool completely, then cut it into 6 squares. Serve a single layer of shortcake with the blackberry mixture on top for 6 servings, or serve a double layer of shortcake with the blackberry mixture between the layers for 3 servings. Top with the Coconut Whipped Cream (if using).

DARK CHOCOLATE *Bread Pudding*

This Louisiana-style dish typically involves leftover bread and a sweet sauce of some kind. In my vegan version, I've added dark chocolate, which essentially replaces the eggs and creates a fudgy and decadent custard. It will have you wishing you could fill an entire swimming pool with it and gulp your way through it. Or at least that's how I feel about it.

Serves: 6

5–6 cups (175–210 g) diced crusty vegan bread

3 cups (720 ml) nondairy milk

½ cup (120 ml) pure maple syrup

¼ cup (48 g) vegan sugar

2 tsp (10 ml) pure vanilla extract

1 tbsp (7 g) cocoa powder

½ tsp salt

1½ cups (270 g) finely chopped vegan dark chocolate, divided

1 tsp solid coconut oil

Vegan vanilla ice cream, vegan powdered sugar or Coconut Whipped Cream (page 151; optional)

Preheat the oven to 350°F (177°C).

Place the bread in a 13 x 9–inch (33 x 23–cm) baking dish. Spread the bread out evenly in the bottom of the dish.

In a large saucepan over medium heat, whisk together the milk, maple syrup, sugar, vanilla, cocoa powder and salt. Bring the mixture to a simmer, reduce the heat to low and add ½ cup (90 g) of the chocolate. Whisk just to melt the chocolate, then remove the saucepan from the heat.

Pour the chocolate mixture over the bread and press the bread down into the chocolate, making sure the bread is saturated in the chocolate.

Let the bread sit for about 5 minutes so it can soak up the chocolate mixture.

Bake the bread pudding for 30 to 40 minutes, or until the chocolate has firmed up but is still fudgy looking.

Let the bread pudding cool for about 5 minutes while you make the melted chocolate topping.

In the same saucepan used to make the chocolate custard, heat the remaining 1 cup (180 g) of chocolate over low heat. Heat just until the chocolate has melted, stirring the whole time. Remove the saucepan from the heat and stir in the coconut oil.

Drizzle the chocolate topping over the bread pudding. Serve it warm with the ice cream, powdered sugar or Coconut Whipped Cream (if using).

KEY LIME PIE *Bars*

Fun fact: I have a giant slice of Key lime pie tattooed on my arm. So, it is safe to assume I'm pretty into Key lime pie. Over the years I have tried to make many, many variations of vegan Key lime pie, trying to match the taste and texture of the dairy-based version as much as possible. After tweaking this recipe five times, these dessert bars are making me proud!

Serves: 16 to 20

GRAHAM CRACKER CRUST

2½ cups (225 g) vegan graham cracker crumbs

3 tbsp (27 g) vegan brown sugar

1 cup (240 g) vegan butter, melted

KEY LIME PIE FILLING

1 cup (240 ml) Key lime or lime juice

2 (15-oz [450-ml]) cans full-fat coconut milk or coconut cream

1 cup (192 g) vegan granulated sugar

1½ tsp (5 g) lime zest

¼ tsp salt

6 tbsp (54 g) cornstarch

Coconut Whipped Cream (page 151) or store-bought vegan whipped topping (optional)

To make the graham cracker crust, preheat the oven to 350°F (177°C). Spray a 13 x 9–inch (33 x 23–cm) baking pan with nonstick cooking spray.

In a large bowl, stir together the graham cracker crumbs and brown sugar. Pour the butter into the bowl and stir to coat all the crumbs in the butter. Make sure the graham cracker crumbs are moist—they should stick together if you squeeze them.

Press the graham cracker crumbs evenly into the bottom of the prepared baking pan. (I like to use the bottom of a cup to press them down firmly.)

Bake the crust for 12 to 15 minutes, or until it is brown and firm.

While the crust bakes, make the Key lime pie filling. In a medium saucepan over medium-high heat, whisk together the Key lime juice, coconut milk, sugar, lime zest and salt. Continue whisking until the mixture is homogenous.

Add the cornstarch to the saucepan. Whisk to combine, making sure there are no lumps, for 3 to 5 minutes.

Bring the mixture to a simmer, reduce the heat to low and simmer for 3 to 5 minutes, whisking frequently, until the filling is thick. Remove the saucepan from the heat.

When the crust is done, remove it from the oven. Pour the filling into the crust and smooth it out evenly. Let the crust and filling cool for about 15 minutes, then put the baking dish in the fridge for at least 4 hours to chill the filling. (The filling will look soupy at first, but it will get firm and creamy once it has cooled.)

Cut the Key lime pie into bars into 2 x 2–inch (5 x 5–cm) squares and serve them with the Coconut Whipped Cream (if using).

BANANA *Pudding Cups*

When I was a kid, I hated pudding. It was the only sweet treat I would ever turn down—until the most drool-worthy banana pudding was put in front of me at a family gathering. It turns out that it was the texture that bothered me about pudding. However, adding the glorious complexity of cookies, bananas and whipped cream was something I could get behind. This is an ode to the beauty of a classic banana pudding, and this plant-based version does not disappoint! To make this dessert even easier, feel free to use store-bought vegan whipped cream instead of making your own.

Serves: 4 to 6

VANILLA PUDDING

2 cups (480 ml) cold soy or almond milk

3 tbsp (27 g) cornstarch

¼ cup (48 g) vegan granulated sugar

1 tbsp (15 ml) pure vanilla extract

Pinch of salt

COCONUT WHIPPED CREAM

1 (14-oz [420-ml]) can full-fat coconut milk or coconut cream, chilled

¼ cup (33 g) vegan powdered sugar

Pinch of salt

PUDDING CUPS

8–10 vegan graham crackers

2 medium bananas, thinly sliced

To make the vanilla pudding, whisk together the milk and cornstarch in a small bowl, making sure the cornstarch has dissolved completely in the milk.

Transfer the milk mixture to a small saucepan. Add the sugar. Heat the mixture over medium-high heat, whisking to combine the ingredients. Cook for 1 to 2 minutes.

Add the vanilla and salt. Bring the mixture to a simmer and reduce the heat to low. Simmer for 3 to 4 minutes, whisking frequently, until the pudding is thick.

Remove the pudding from the heat and let it cool for 5 minutes. Put the pudding in the fridge to chill for about 30 minutes, or until the pudding is thick and firm. (If you chill the pudding for a long time, it will get really thick; just whisk it to make it smooth and fluffy again.)

When the pudding is ready, make the coconut whipped cream. Scoop out only the thick, creamy part of the coconut milk that is at the top of the can into the bowl of stand mixer or a large bowl. Reserve the liquid for another use.

Beat the coconut cream at high speed for 3 to 5 minutes, until it starts to thicken. Sprinkle in the powdered sugar and salt. Whip until the mixture is thick, 4 to 5 minutes.

To make the pudding cups, crumble a graham cracker into the bottom of a serving cup. Then add a layer of sliced bananas, then a layer of vanilla pudding. Add more graham crackers and more bananas, then top the pudding cup with whipped coconut cream. Garnish the pudding cup with a slice of banana and a few more graham cracker crumbs.

Repeat the preceding steps to create as many pudding cups as you want.

BERRY-PEACH CORNMEAL *Cobbler*

This incredible union of berries, peaches and a sweet cornmeal topping makes the world a better place. There is something so comforting to me about serving this cobbler hot, with the warm berries, juicy peaches and crunchy-on-the-outside, soft-on-the-inside dough on top. Serve this cobbler with your favorite nondairy vanilla ice cream. That hot and cold combo will be the best thing to happen to you all day.

Serves: 6 to 8

FILLING

2 cups (200 g) fresh blueberries

2 cups (288 g) fresh blackberries

2 cups (288 g) fresh raspberries

2 cups (450 g) sliced fresh peaches

3 tbsp (27 g) cornstarch

½ cup (96 g) vegan sugar

2 tbsp (30 ml) fresh lemon juice

TOPPING

2 cups (240 g) all-purpose flour

½ cup (85 g) cornmeal

1½ tsp (6 g) baking powder

¼ cup (48 g) vegan sugar

1 tsp salt

½ cup (120 g) solid coconut oil

¾ cup (180 ml) nondairy milk

Coarse vegan sugar (optional)

Vegan ice cream (optional)

Preheat the oven to 400°F (204°C). Spray an 11 x 7–inch (28 x 18–cm) baking dish with nonstick cooking spray.

To make the filling, combine the blueberries, blackberries, raspberries and peaches in a large bowl.

Sprinkle the cornstarch, sugar and lemon juice on top of the fruit. Toss to fully coat the fruit.

Transfer the fruit to the prepared baking dish. Set the baking dish aside.

To make the topping, sift the flour in a large bowl. Stir in the cornmeal, baking powder, sugar and salt. Stir to fully combine.

Break the coconut oil up into small pieces with your hands. Drop the coconut oil into the flour mixture. Work the coconut oil into the flour mixture with your fingers until it is evenly distributed and the mixture resembles sand.

Add the milk to the flour mixture a little at a time, stirring to combine. The topping should be the texture and consistency of a biscuit dough.

Drop large mounds of the dough on top of the fruit, covering most of the top of the fruit. Sprinkle the top of the dough with the coarse sugar (if using).

Bake the cobbler for 30 to 40 minutes, or until the dough is baked through and brown on top.

Serve the cobbler warm with the ice cream (if using).

Hot Tip: This recipe works great with any kind of fruit you want to use. Use the same amount of fruit called for in the ingredients. I love to use apples in the fall!

ACKNOWLEDGMENTS

My career and my life would not be possible without all the people I have in my corner. There are many people who've got my back no matter what. Let me say, I am one lucky girl! Let me take a moment to talk about the people in my life, the people I can't live without.

Julie Grace. I'm not sure the words exist to properly explain how amazing this woman is. She is on my permanent staff and keeps Rabbit and Wolves going, handling all the daily tasks that need to be done. This book would not have been possible without her. She edited photos, she proofread, she let me bounce all my ideas off her, she told me I was doing a great job even when I felt like my work wasn't good enough. Her strengths are my weaknesses and life wouldn't be okay without her at my side. Not only is she the greatest employee of all time, we have been friends for ten years. We've been through everything together, and I wouldn't have it any other way. There is no one I trust more to do the best work and to be there to listen to me. There is no one else like her in the world, and I love her to death. She emits beauty, in every form, out into the world—I am so much better for knowing her.

Chris, my husband. I don't know how much other people like their husbands, but not only am I in love with my husband but I also really, really like him. I would rather spend the day hanging out with him doing nothing than anything else. Chris is behind me always. When I wanted to be a full-time food blogger, which sounded crazy to most people, it didn't sound crazy to Chris. He has never doubted me, not for a second. He completely jumped on board when I told him I was going to write a book. Every day, he says, "Tell me what you need, and I will take care of it." Buying groceries, arranging props, washing dishes, entertaining our daughter—anything I ask for, he makes it happen. He also has a great palate: He eats meat and he loves my food, so I consider that a good endorsement. There is no one else in the world I want to do life with, so I'm pretty happy with my decision to do life with him.

Ethan, Zach and Tia, my siblings. We may not have had much growing up, but we've always had each other. My brothers and sister are constantly telling me that what I'm doing is amazing and how proud they are. I don't care a lot about other people's opinions, but I care about theirs. They are my heart, and their support can get me through anything.

Ken, my dad. He's the best. He's beyond intelligent, he's beyond loving, he always knows what to do, and he is just the coolest. There has not been one second that I can remember him questioning what I wanted to do. He has always said he wants me to be happy and that I need to figure out what makes me happy. When I told him I wanted to be a food blogger, he was totally on board. My dad is who I call if I just want to talk and he is also who I call if I need advice. He has only ever made me feel loved, and he deserves all the greatest things in the world!

Lenore, my daughter. She gives me purpose. Before she was born, I was a lost twenty-something with a love of food, a culinary degree and no direction. She gave me that direction. I wanted to show her what I could do. I wanted her to be proud of me. She completes our little family and I love her more than I thought was possible.

My mother-in-law, Joann. She's a big reason I am where I am today. She gives my family so much support. She's believed in me every step of the way. She makes my recipes, she tells everyone she talks to about me. I owe a lot of what I am to her. Without her, it would not be possible for me to scale the mountains I keep climbing.

Page Street Publishing. They made my dreams come true. Writing a cookbook has been my dream since childhood. I pretended to have my own cooking show in the kitchen when no one was watching. I came up with some really great commercials for my fake cookbook that I would advertise on my fake cooking show. This book is something I've fantasized about my whole life. Page Street found me, and I am thankful every day that they took a chance on me!

Everyone who has taste-tested, encouraged me, held me together, told me everything would be all right, told me I was good enough, told me that I could do this. This book is for all of you. Thank you.

ABOUT THE AUTHOR

Lauren Boehme Hartmann is the founder, recipe developer and photographer behind the incredibly successful food blog Rabbit and Wolves. Born and raised in Florida, Lauren sprang forth into this world with an insatiable hunger and has been eating nonstop ever since. Lauren graduated from culinary school in 2007 and still fondly remembers all the mother sauces she had to make. She is passionate about not eating animals, listening to true crime podcasts, reading and watching horror movies. She literally giggles with joy when someone tells her that her recipes make it easy to be vegan. She has built her life around creating unique vegan recipes and pushing the envelope with what can be made vegan. She suffers from PTSD and cooking is incredibly therapeutic for her; she is happiest when she can be creative and make things beautiful and delicious. She wants to do nothing else in life but create vegan recipes to share with the world. Lauren lives in Florida with her husband, Chris, and their daughter, Lenore.

INDEX